100 Ideas for Primary Teachers: Writing

Other titles in the 100 Ideas for Primary Teachers series:

100 Ideas for Primary Teachers: Developing Thinking Skills
by Steve Bowkett

100 Ideas for Primary Teachers: Behaviour Management
by Molly Potter

100 Ideas for Primary Teachers: Outstanding Teaching
by Stephen Lockyer

100 Ideas for Primary Teachers: Transition to Secondary School
by Molly Potter

100 Ideas for Primary Teachers: Supporting Children with Dyslexia
by Gavin Reid and Shannon Green

100 Ideas for Primary Teachers: Raising Boys' Achievement
by Gary Wilson

100 Ideas for Primary Teachers: Homework
by Jenna Lucas

100 Ideas for Primary Teachers: Mindfulness in the Classroom
by Tammie Prince

100 Ideas for Primary Teachers: Literacy
by Rob Smith and Katherine Simpson

100 Ideas for Primary Teachers: Engaging Parents
by Janet Goodall and Kathryn Weston

100 Ideas for Primary Teachers: History
by Clare Horrie and Rachel Hillman

100 Ideas for Primary Teachers: Questioning
by Peter Worley

100 Ideas for Primary Teachers: Supporting Pupils with Autism
by Francine Brower

100 Ideas for Primary Teachers: Supporting Pupils with Social, Emotional and Mental Health Difficulties
by Roy Howarth

100 Ideas for Primary Teachers: Outdoor Learning
by Adam Bushnell and Sc.out.ed

100 Ideas for Primary Teachers:

Writing

Adam Bushnell, Rob Smith
and David Waugh

BLOOMSBURY EDUCATION
LONDON OXFORD NEW YORK NEW DELHI SYDNEY

BLOOMSBURY EDUCATION
Bloomsbury Publishing Plc
50 Bedford Square, London, WC1B 3DP, UK

BLOOMSBURY, BLOOMSBURY EDUCATION and the Diana logo are trademarks of Bloomsbury Publishing Plc

First published in Great Britain, 2020

A catalogue record for this book is available from the British Library

ISBN: PB: 978-1-4729-7236-1; ePDF: 978-1-4729-7239-2;
ePub: 978-1-4729-7238-5

2 4 6 8 10 9 7 5 3 1 (paperback)

Typeset by Newgen KnowledgeWorks Pvt. Ltd., Chennai, India
Printed and bound in the UK by CPI Group (UK) Ltd, Croydon CR0 4YY

All papers used by Bloomsbury Publishing Plc are natural, recyclable products from wood grown in well managed forests. The manufacturing processes conform to the environmental regulations of the country of origin

To find out more about our authors and books visit www.bloomsbury.com and sign up for our newsletters

Acknowledgements: To our friends and family for all of their continued support.

Contents

Introduction

This book has been written by people who regularly teach writing in primary schools and teach about writing to professional educators. The lesson ideas are all tried and tested and have been used successfully with children.

We firmly believe that good writing is built upon speaking, listening and reading. It is important that children have lots of examples of high-quality texts available so that they can see what good writing looks like and can appreciate differing styles and genres. Discussion about texts should include a focus on vocabulary and phrasing, as well as structure, grammar and syntax. Through discussing vocabulary, we can focus on spelling patterns, etymology and morphology so that children develop their language knowledge and learn how to apply what they learn to new words and phrases.

Writing lessons should not be dominated by children seeking help with spelling. Rather, teachers should be able to discuss writing with individuals, groups and sometimes the whole class. When problems arise, it can be valuable to stop work and discuss them while giving everyone new ideas for vocabulary and phrasing.

It is important, too, that we model writing for children through shared writing, with the teacher scribing, thinking aloud and composing text as children watch, discuss and contribute their own ideas. Sharing our own writing with children shows them that writing is a valuable and important life skill and not just something they have to do at school. As Lev Vygotsky (1978, page 118) argued: '...writing should be incorporated into a task that is necessary and relevant for life'.

Vygotsky also asserted that learners can achieve more when guided by an experienced teacher and his concept of the 'zone of proximal development' describes how what children can do initially with adult support will later be possible independently.

We have a responsibility to *teach* writing as opposed to simply responding to it through marking and comments. It is important that we make it purposeful by providing real audiences for children's work, including other classes, parents and carers, and other teachers. We hope you will use our ideas as starting points for a wealth of stimulating writing activities which will ensure that writing is regarded by pupils as a pleasure rather than a chore.

*Vygotsky, L. (1978), *Mind in Society: The Development of Higher Psychological Processes.* Cambridge, MA: Harvard University Press.

How to use this book

This book includes quick, easy and practical ideas for you to dip in and out of to support you in providing exciting and engaging activities to develop pupils' writing skills.

Each idea includes:

- a catchy title, easy to refer to and share with your colleagues
- an interesting quote linked to the idea
- a summary of the idea in bold, making it easy to flick through the book and identify an idea you want to use at a glance
- a step-by-step guide to implementing the idea.

Each idea also includes one or more of the following:

Teaching tip

Practical tips and advice for how and how not to run the activity or put the idea into practice.

Taking it further

Ideas and advice for how to extend the idea or develop it further.

Bonus idea ★

There are 28 bonus ideas in this book that are extra-exciting, extra-original and extra-interesting.

Share how you use these ideas and find out what other practitioners have done using **#100ideas**.

Traditional tales and monstrous myths

IDEA 1

Myths in minutes

'Myths and legends is my topic. What do I do? There are just too many of them!'

Children use common features of myths such as a hero, a monster and a triadic structure to write their own myths.

Taking it further

This basic myth structure is adaptable and could be changed into a play script that the children then act out in small groups. It could also be retold as a newspaper report with headlines such as 'Davideus defeats deadly demon!' or 'Robeus marries the princess!' Other retellings could be done as diary entries from the perspective of the hero or flashback stories from the perspective of the monster.

Monsters feature in myths from all over the world and they're usually crazy-looking creatures! To make a myth, ask the children to first design a monster. It could be a multi-headed animal like a two-headed snake, or it could have many legs like the sea monster, the kraken. The monster's appearance can then be described. As these monsters tend to wreak havoc by destroying buildings or kidnapping royalty, their actions can also be described.

Once the monster is made, then a hero character should be selected to defeat the monster. This character can be a king, queen, prince, princess, lord, lady or some other posh person. Usually a reward is offered too.

The hero can be a boy, girl, man or woman. In Ancient Greece, girls were often given names that ended in 'a' in honour of the goddesses Hera or Athena. Boys' names often ended in 'eus' in honour of Zeus, the king of the gods. So, children could use their own names but add 'a' or 'eus' to the ending. There could be Emilya or Barackeus, for example.

These myths often follow rules of three, known as a triadic structure. So perhaps the hero attempts to kill the monster but fails, tries again and fails, but succeeds on the third attempt. Or the hero uses three weapons or three magical items to kill the monster, such as an ice shield, a fire sword or flying boots.

Little Rabbit Foo Foo

'What's a goonie anyway?'

Children rewrite the traditional tale by keeping the structure but replacing the setting.

'Little Rabbit Foo Foo' is the tale of a psychotic rabbit that bops mice, worms, tigers and goblins on the head. Each time, the Good Fairy comes down and warns the rabbit that if he carries on, she will turn him into a goonie. She gives him three chances but in the end the rabbit becomes a goonie.

Invite children to rewrite the story using the following ideas. They can tell the new story orally before writing it down.

- Ask the children to choose a different small and cute animal, such as a kitten, duckling or ladybird. The new bad character could be named in a similar style to Little Rabbit Foo Foo, such as Little Kitten Fluff Fluff.
- This change of character might lead to a different setting from the forest, such as under the sea, or on a frozen landscape.
- The children then need to choose a good character, such as a wizard, genie or fairy.
- After that, four characters are needed as victims. These could be animals that live in the children's chosen settings. So, if they have chosen under the sea, they might have a crab, a squid, a mermaid and a seahorse.
- Their bad character then does something to these victims, such as flicking their noses, pushing them or even giving them wedgies.
- Each time, the good character warns the bad character that they will be turned into something, such as slime, stone or a sausage.

Teaching tip

Children love the comedy violence, but they also enjoy the repetition and clear structure of the story. It is a story that easily lends itself to audience participation as it follows a set pattern, like many traditional tales, of the rule of three. Three chances to change are offered and then no more.

Taking it further

Include dialogue at each stage of the retelling. Ask the children to use inverted commas and a range of synonyms for 'said' with a variety of adverbs. For example: '"Little Kitten Fluff Fluff, you have three chances or I'll turn you into slime!" called the Good Witch sternly.'

IDEA 3

Legendary creatures

'I'm so sick and tired of my class going on and on about unicorns!'

Children describe creatures of legends such as dragons, mermaids or unicorns using nouns, adjectives, verbs and adverbs.

Collect images or, even better, toy figures of creatures from legends such as dragons, mermaids or unicorns. You could also use more unusual creatures such as banshees, harpies or fairies. Ask the children to choose one of these creatures to describe.

Give the children a picture of their chosen creature with plenty of space around it to write about it. Ask them to name the body parts of the creature using nouns such as 'head', 'eyes', 'teeth', 'skin', 'scales', 'feathers', 'claws', 'tail', and so on. Then these nouns can be given shades of colour, such as 'forest green scales', 'blood red eyes' or 'crystal white horns'. More adjectives can then be added to describe the size, shape, texture and general look of the creature, such as 'menacing', 'enticing' or 'awesome'.

Then ask the children what this creature does. Is it kind and caring? Is it evil and destructive? This will lead to writing verbs for the creature such as 'singing', 'gliding', 'galloping', 'tearing', 'devouring' or 'destroying'.

Adverbs can then be added to the verbs such as 'singing beautifully', 'gliding gracefully', 'galloping speedily' or 'destroying wildly'.

After all the nouns, adjectives, verbs and adverbs have been collected, the children can write sentences based on their vocabulary banks. There could be sentences such as 'The ocean-blue, graceful sea dragon was gliding smoothly over the waves' or 'Loudly, the deadly, vicious creature was stomping, roaring and snarling toward the castle.'

Teaching tip

Use Alison Wilcox's *Descriptosaurus* to add to the children's collections of nouns, adjectives, verbs and adverbs.

Taking it further

Ask the children to score their creatures on ratings such as power, strength, flexibility and size, and to make cards in the style of Top Trumps™. These cards could be used as a game for the classroom.

Wilcox, A. (2018), *Descriptosaurus: Supporting Creative Writing for Ages 8-14* (3rd edn.). Abingdon: Routledge.

Fables

'Slow and steady wins the race!'

Children write a story that teaches the reader something, by including an ending such as 'that is why you shouldn't text and drive' or 'she never posted mean things online ever again'.

Fables such as *The Tortoise and the Hare* are teaching stories. In that particular story we are reminded of the perils of boasting. In *The Ant and the Grasshopper* we are taught the virtues of planning ahead. Fables are meant to teach a moral.

Ask the children what lessons they could teach younger children. It might be something like always holding hands with your family when crossing the road or always showing good manners.

The animals in fables often fit the story. The speedy hare is boastful, the steady tortoise is tenacious and the bouncing grasshopper is hyper. Ask the children to choose an animal that fits their moral. A hedgehog might never want to hold hands when crossing a road and a shark may never show good manners.

Begin to think of consequences to these actions. For example, the hedgehog ends up squashed (but not dead!) and the shark has no friends. The animal eventually learns its lesson and never behaves in that way again. So, you end up with a basic narrative like this:

> *There was once a magpie who used to pull leaves off trees with its beak. One sunny day it pulled every leaf from every tree in the park where it lived. That night a cold wind blew through the park. The magpie huddled, shivering in its nest but without the leaves for shelter. From the very next day the magpie never pulled a single leaf off any tree.*

Teaching tip

These fables can be expanded with descriptions once they are completed. More advanced vocabulary can then be added as well as improved sentence openers.

IDEA 5

Mythical monsters

Hagrid: 'Who told you 'bout Fluffy?'
Ron: 'Fluffy?!'
Hermione: 'That thing has a name?'
(*Harry Potter and the Philosopher's Stone*, film)

Children make new creatures by mixing animals together, similar to the Chimera from Ancient Greece, the Sphinx from Ancient Egypt or the Cockatrice (which was first described in 14th-century literature).

Monsters feature heavily in myths from all over the world. The Chimera has the head of a lion, body of a goat and tail of a snake. The Sphinx has the head of a human, body of a lion and wings like an eagle. The Cockatrice is a dragon with a rooster's head.

Give the children dice and ask them to circle which animal they get for each part of their monster.

Your monster will have the head of a...

1	2	3	4	5	6
crocodile	shark	lion	dragon	snake	eagle

Your monster will have the body of a...

1	2	3	4	5	6
wolf	vulture	giraffe	horse	bear	monkey

Your monster will have the arms of a...

1	2	3	4	5	6
gorilla	T-Rex	tiger	dog	crab	octopus

Your monster will have the legs of a...

1	2	3	4	5	6
chicken	jellyfish	zebra	cat	pig	elephant

Your monster will have the tail of a...

1	2	3	4	5	6
lizard	fish	skunk	fox	squirrel	scorpion

The monster can then be drawn and described. But it may also have powers based on elements like ice, lightning or poison. The Chimera can breathe fire like a dragon and the Cockatrice can turn people to stone like Medusa from Greek mythology. These monsters may give inspiration to the children or the children may want to come up with their own powers to write about.

Taking it further

Take photocopies of the monsters the children have created and make a class flipbook, where children can 'flip' the heads, bodies or tails to make a vast range of new monsters.

Creation stories

'In the beginning...'

Children write stories to explain the origins of animals, such as 'How the Rabbit got Long Ears', 'Why the Turtle has a Shell' or 'How the Giraffe got a Long Neck'.

Creation or origin stories are among the oldest in the world. They were used to help people make sense of the world, such as why the sea has salt, what makes thunder and lightning or how rainbows are formed. But they were also to explain the origin of why animals look the way they do, such as how the parrot got its colours, why the birds sing and how the cheetah got so fast.

Ask the children to choose an animal and write down the most distinguishing feature of that animal. In other words, what is the first thing they notice about that animal? It might be a hyena's laugh, a lion's mane or a rooster's comb. This then becomes the title of their creation story, such as 'How the Hyena got its Laugh', 'Why the Lion has a Mane' or 'Why the Rooster has a Comb on its Head'.

Children now know the beginning of their story: the animal looks different from the way it looks today. But perhaps the animal also had a problem in some way. The hyena might have always been grumpy, the lion might have been cold and the rooster might have looked dull.

Children also know the ending of their story: the animal looks the way it looks today. Perhaps this makes the animal happy and we have a happy ending.

But it is the middle of the story that requires the most thought. As with other myths, these stories can follow the rule of three. Three major

Taking it further

Create creation stories based on nature, such as 'Why the Grass is Green', 'Where Wind First Formed' or 'Why the Moon Comes Out at Night'.

events lead the animal to look the way it does today. The grumpy hyena might be told a joke that doesn't make it laugh, is then told another unsuccessful joke, but finally is told the funniest joke it has ever heard and still keeps laughing about it today.

Perhaps the lion was cold so tried covering its head with leaves but these blew away. It then put a bush on its head but this was too itchy, so it finally drinks a magic potion from a witch which gives it a thick mane of hair.

Or the rooster is jealous of the other animals with their horns, antlers and other decorative headwear, so he adds some branches to his head but these end up snapping. He then places flowers in his feathers around his head but these wither away. Finally he prays to the god of the birds to make him look more beautiful than all of the other animals and wakes up the next day with a bright red comb. He cock-a-doodle-doos in triumph every morning ever since.

God-like deities often feature in these stories and can provide a convenient quick-fix ending.

Bonus idea ★

See the TV show *Tinga Tinga Tales* on the CBeebies website and on YouTube. There are many examples of animated animal creation stories on there to use as a model.

IDEA 7

Fairy Land

'Nobody ever sends postcards anymore!'

Children write postcards from a visit to a fairytale land where fishes fly and birds swim in the sea.

Fairy doors can be bought very cheaply but can be a valuable resource in the classroom. It's recommended to install the door quite high up so that you can reach it but the children can't. Nothing ruins the magic of a fairy door more than a child pulling it from the wall!

When a fairy door magically appears in the classroom there can be quite a lot of excitement, particularly when a letter or postcard accompanies the arrival of the door. This can be typed with a small font size before being printed off, cut out and secreted near the door. A magnifying glass may be necessary to read the writing but this adds to the authenticity of the experience.

The postcard may be a simple greeting from the residents of Fairy Land, letting the children know what they have been up to. Or it may describe a recent event, such as a spell that went wrong.

The postcard could go on to describe some of the animals in Fairy Land, which may be like animals in our world but behave rather differently. The fishes might fly and birds might swim, or there could be fire-breathing dogs, ice-skating hamsters or trampolining hippos.

The children could then write their own postcards from Fairy Land, imagining they had been to visit and following the same pattern in the narrative. They could begin with a greeting, describe the setting, say what they did on their visit and finally describe what the animals were doing there.

Teaching tip

Invent magical addresses for where the fairies live, such as Mushroom House, Glitterwood Lane, Fairy Land, MGC WND.

Big Bad Wolf

'I'll huff and I'll puff and I'll blow your school down!' (*The Three Little Pigs*)

Children describe a trap that could be used to catch the Big Bad Wolf if he came to school.

When the Big Bad Wolf is hungry he stops at nothing to find his food. From dressing up as Grandma to climbing down chimneys, he is relentless. Imagine if the Big Bad Wolf came to school. How could the building be secured? What could be used to barricade the doors and windows? What would happen if he still got in?

Ask the children if they can design a trap to catch the Big Bad Wolf. However, the trap must be constructed using only school equipment. The PE cupboard can be a source of inspiration, with skipping ropes, nets for goals and large, heavy mats as possible parts of the trap. But look beyond this and take a look around the whole of the school, both inside and out, for other possibilities. Can climbing frames be incorporated? What about tables, chairs and other classroom furniture?

The children can then label the trap and use nouns like 'lure', 'bait' and 'spring lock' but also adjectives such as 'secure', 'strong' and 'bolted'. Explanation texts can then be written not only describing the actual trap but also explaining how to construct it and how to catch a wolf by luring it into the trap. The best hiding places can be described too, such as inside cupboards, under desks, on top of the school roof or even behind the dinner staff.

Taking it further

If the wolf has been trapped then how could the children teach him to be good? After that they could imagine what job the wolf might do in their school, such as caretaker, dinner staff or headteacher. What would school be like then?

Bonus idea ★

Ask the children to design a trap for home (this idea may involve parental help). The trap should be like the school one but constructed using only equipment found in the home.

Giant descriptions

'Fee-fi-fo-fum, I smell the blood of an Englishman!' (*Jack and the Beanstalk*)

This activity involves describing giants, including the nonsense language that they use, but asking children to change the first letter with another consonant, so 'Fee-fi-fo-fum' becomes, for example, 'Bee-bi-bo-bum'.

The one thing giants all have in common is their size. Adjectives to replace 'big' can be used but there are also opportunities to compare size using similes, to suggest size using metaphors and to exaggerate size with hyperbole.

Ask children to design and describe a giant. The children could describe giants with horns, scales, wings or oversized earlobes. As well as a frost giant from Norse mythology there could be fire giants, sea giants or jungle giants. As they are such varied creatures, children can let their imaginations run wild and have any kind of giant they like.

In *Jack and the Beanstalk* the famous line, 'Fee-fi-fo-fum, I smell the blood of an Englishman' is spoken by the giant. 'Fee-fi-fo-fum' is nonsense verse that contains alliteration. If the children replace the 'f' with another consonant then they can make their own nonsense verse for their own giant. There could be 'See-si-so-sum', 'Wee-wi-wo-wum' or 'Bee-bi-bo-bum'.

As well as describing what the giant looks like and says, children can then go on to describe the actions of the giant. What does he or she do? Is the giant good or bad?

In *Jack and the Beanstalk* the giant lives in a castle up in the clouds. The children can then go on to describe where their giant lives.

Taking it further

What precious objects could there be inside the giant's home? Instead of a goose that lays golden eggs there could be a donkey that sneezes golden coins, a lizard that lays diamond eggs or a cow that shoots fire from its udders. The children could describe the inside of the home as well as the outside.

Fairytale Olympics

'Ready, steady... go!'

Children select fairytale characters to compete in Olympic sports. For example, the Gingerbread Man does the 100 m sprint.

Summer and winter Olympic sports are diverse and numerous. So are fairytale characters! Matching a fairytale character to an Olympic sport can be an entertaining way of describing a particular event. Some characters lend themselves easily to a sport, for example, Ariel the mermaid to artistic swimming or Puss in Boots to fencing. But perhaps it is the mismatching of characters to a particular sport that children would enjoy writing about the most. For example, Little Red Riding Hood on a BMX bike, an ogre figure skating or Granny trampolining.

The BBC's Rio 2016 Olympics advert shows rainforest animals competing in Olympic summer sports, such as synchronised-swimming crocodiles and a weightlifting armadillo. This might give the children some ideas for their own Fairytale Olympics.

FIFA's 2010 World Cup promotional video shows animals playing football. This too might help children to describe not just the characters but the step-by-step action of their chosen sport, from the poetic movement of figure-skating unicorns to the intense action of a boxing match between Rapunzel and Snow White.

Shorter sentences create a sense of urgency and excitement, particularly when the sport reaches its climax, such as the moment when a ski jumper reaches their highest point. Each part of the sport can be described but with the extra twist of this being a fairytale event.

Teaching tip

By listening to some examples of Olympic sports commentary, the children can also get an idea of the tone to use in their writing.

Taking it further

The children could create their own Olympics advert like the BBC one, which they could act out with friends and narrate.

Structured poetry

Metaphor poetry

'Aren't metaphors just similes but without the "like"?'

Children describe an animal using metaphors in a structured way, using colours, the weather, sports and more.

Taking it further

Ask the children to use the same descriptive techniques but instead of an animal, describe a vehicle, hobby or even a family member or friend.

Ask the children to choose one of their favourite animals to write about. It can be from the sea, the sky or anywhere else. It can be a living animal or one that is extinct or even mythical.

Ask the children to write their animal's name and then the word 'is' (for example, 'hamster is' or 'dog is'). Then explain what a metaphor is. The Kids Wordsmyth Online Dictionary definition is 'a phrase that describes something by comparing it to some other thing'. It is worth pointing out that a metaphor can also be defined like this but instead of the thing being 'like' something else, it 'is' something else. For example, 'my sister is a nightmare', 'my teacher is a dragon' or 'the storm was an angry monster'.

After the word 'is' the children then write down a colour for their animal. It's not literally the colour of the animal but rather the colour they think of when they picture the animal in their mind. It could be 'hamster is gold', 'unicorn is rainbow' or 'shark is black'.

Then ask the children to think of which weather best suits their animal. It could be 'dog is the sunshine', 'eagle is a storm' or 'pig is wind'.

Next, ask the children to choose which sport fits their animal. It might be 'cat is gymnastics', 'lion is football' or 'gorilla is wrestling'.

This same technique can be used to describe the animal as one of their favourite things, such as a video game, YouTuber or book.

I am a dragon

'I am a dragon with huge teeth... I can bite you... GNASH!'

Children write a poem that describes a dragon's body part and then an action that goes with it. They use onomatopoeia to describe the sounds the dragon makes.

Give the children a picture of a dragon. Ask them to label it with nouns, for example, 'teeth', 'claws', 'wings', 'eyes', 'horns', and so on. Then ask the children to add verbs to explain what the dragon does with each body part, such as 'bite', 'scratch', 'stare', 'fly' and 'stab'.

Next give the children a template of: 'I am a dragon with _______. I can _______.' Repeat this several times. Ask the children to add their own nouns and verbs for what the dragon looks like and what it does with each body part.

The word 'onomatopoeia' comes from the combination of two Greek words, *'onoma'* meaning name and *'poiein'* meaning to make. This means onomatopoeia is where a word means the sound it makes. The word 'boing', for example, is a sound effect as well as being a noun or a verb. Ask the children to add sounds after their verbs so you end up with a poem that follows this structure:

I am a dragon with HUGE TEETH.
I can BITE YOU... GNASH!
I am a dragon with A SPIKY BACK.
I can FLIP OVER AND SQUISH YOU... SPLAT!
I am a dragon with A GIANT TAIL.
I can WHACK YOU OUT OF THE WAY...
WHOOSH!
I am a dragon with FLAMING BREATH.
I can BURN YOU... SIZZLE!
I am a dragon with A DEADLY BITE.
I can KILL YOU... SNAP!

Teaching tip

Encourage the children to read their writing as a performance poem. They should call out the sound effect so that the onomatopoeia is emphasised.

IDEA 13

Shakespeare raps

'How do I compare thee to hip hop?'

Children write poems in iambic pentameter that can be rapped as a performance poem.

Taking it further

Use a drum, such as a djembe, to sound out the number of syllables in words. Start with names such as one syllable in Ben, two in Mia and three in Hasina.

Iambic pentameter uses ten syllables in each line and is accented on every second beat. It's sometimes known as the 'Da Dum' rhythm because it sounds like a heart beating in twos:

Da Dum, Da Dum, Da Dum, Da Dum,
Da Dum.

So, in William Shakespeare's *Romeo and Juliet* we have the lines:

Two households, both alike in dignity,
In fair Verona, where we lay our scene,
From ancient grudge break to new mutiny,
Where civil blood makes civil hands unclean.

When Shakespeare wrote in iambic pentameter he started each line with a capital letter so the reader knew it was important. As a result of this, these iambic pentameter sections in the plays are easy to find.

The verse above also follows an ABAB rhyming pattern, much like modern-day rap music. In fact, as Shakespeare wrote in iambic pentameter with rhyme, these sections of the text are quite simple to rap. If you read the lines from *Romeo and Juliet* above they can be rapped quite easily.

When you ask children to write their own iambic pentameter raps, it's probably the rhyming that they'll find difficult. So give the children rhyming word examples with words that have multiple rhyming options. Don't go for orange, purple or silver! Some better options would be mist, twist, fist; kissed, missed, hissed; day, stay, away, play, grey, pray, way; or bite, night, kite, light, sight, write.

Give the children some examples to get them started, such as:

Two twin towns, both the same passionate place,
In fair Newcastle and in Sunderland,
From ancient grudge that is a real disgrace
There is no point it really should be banned.

It doesn't have to follow the same lines that Shakespeare used though. You can also offer some alternative sentence starters such as:

A long time ago...
A man called Bill was...
I like playing...
Books are awesome...
The sun was shining...

Remember to limit each line to ten syllables. The rhyming pattern could be ABAB but an easier alternative would be AABB. For example:

A long time ago there lived a bad king,
He really was awful, such a mean thing,
He liked to eat and got extremely fat,
He chopped off lots of heads, what a big rat!

Once written, these raps can then be performed by the children to each other.

Bonus idea ★

Watch the rapper Akala perform Shakespeare's 'Sonnet 18' on YouTube for the perfect example.

IDEA 14

Macbeth's witches

'By the pricking of my thumbs, something wicked this way comes!' (Shakespeare, *Macbeth*)

Children rewrite the 'Song of the Witches' with different ingredients for the potion.

The 'Song of the Witches' features in Shakespeare's *Macbeth*. The rhythm of the poem means that it can be rapped quite easily. But it can also be rewritten with different ingredients for the cauldron. So, the original version has lines like this:

Fillet of a fenny snake,
In the cauldron boil and bake;
Eye of newt and toe of frog,
Wool of bat and tongue of dog

But if we give the children a template of the song with lines like this...

Fillet of a ________ snake,
In the cauldron ________ and bake;
Eye of ________ and toe of ________,
Wool of ________ and tongue of ________.

... we get a new 'Song of the Witches' with lines like this:

Fillet of a deadly snake,
In the cauldron shake and bake;
Eye of fish and toe of rat,
Wool of sheep and tongue of cat.

The children don't necessarily need the template and the poem doesn't have to rhyme, but some structure may be necessary to help rewrite this classic verse.

Teaching tip

Keep checking the length of the children's lines. Every line should contain roughly the same number of syllables so that certain lines aren't read too quickly as they're so long, or too slowly as they're so short. You can easily find the complete 'Song of the Witches' online.

Sonnet 18

'Shall I compare thee to a summer's day?' (Shakespeare, 'Sonnet 18')

Children write a love poem based on the famous Shakespearean sonnet 'Sonnet 18', such as 'Sonnet for Fortnite', 'Sonnet for Wi-Fi' or 'Sonnet for My Bed'.

'Sonnet 18' is one of Shakespeare's most famous poems. It's a love poem where the bard says that his love cannot be compared to nature and the weather as they are changeable things, whereas his love is immortal and will never change. The poem may need explaining due to the language of the time it was written in; however, the message is clear: it is a poem of love.

Children may love their family, friends or pets but they also love other things too such as films, TV shows, sports, books, video games, YouTube or even Wi-Fi. Ask the children what it is they love and in pairs get them to tell each other why they love that particular thing.

This can lead to children writing sonnets about the things they love.

For instance, they might write a sonnet such as the following ('Sonnet to Star Wars'):

Shall I compare you to Darth Vader?
You are more awesome than a lightsaber!
Rough winds shake yet another Death Star,
And summer is avoiding the big freak Jar Jar.
At times the sun is blazing Tatooine's sand,
Or often it shines on the Cantina Band.
And Boba Fett is cool, he's a bounty hunter thug,
But Jabba is not, he's a really big slug.
So long as there are Jedi with their power,
So long will this poem be read every hour.

Teaching tip

You could give the children sentence starters based on 'Sonnet 18' to get them started, such as:

- Shall I compare you to...
- You are more...
- Rough winds shake the...
- And summer is...

Taking it further

Use some of Shakespeare's other sonnets and rewrite them in the same way. Sonnets 43, 49 or 116 could work well for this.

IDEA 16

Dragon cinquains

'Cinquain? Don't you put that on apple pie?'

Children create a structured cinquain, starting with a noun, then two adjectives, then three verbs, and so on.

Teaching tip

You can find lots of examples of cinquains online from websites such as www.yourdictionary.com and www.readwritethink.org.

Cinquains were created by the American poet Adelaide Crapsey. A cinquain is a poem that is made up of five lines, which follow this pattern:

- Line one: a noun with two syllables.
- Line two: two adjectives with a total of four syllables.
- Line three: three verbs with a total of six syllables.
- Line four: usually a metaphor phrase consisting of four words with a total of eight syllables.
- Line five: usually a synonym for line four, consisting of a word or two words with a total of two syllables.

The children can write about anything that interests them. They could pick a noun with two syllables such as 'football' or 'reading' to be their first line. They could then create a mind map of adjectives, verbs and metaphor phrases that are associated with that noun. This will help the children to create the rest of their cinquain. An example of this is a dragon cinquain:

Dragon
Huge, gigantic
Stomping, roaring, killing
A hunting machine, relentless
Deadly

Season poetry

'In the depth of winter, I finally learned that within me there lay an invincible summer.' (Albert Camus)

Children use a template to write poems about a season's features, such as its weather, holidays and plants.

Tell the children that they are going to create a poem about a season. Choose a season and ask the children to describe the weather that usually occurs in that season, using adjectives such as 'rainy', 'windy' and 'hot'. They can then write about which holidays and special days feature during that season, such as Easter, Halloween or Diwali.

Next, ask the children what the trees, flowers and other plants look like at that time. They can also write about what things they usually do during that season, such as go to the park, have snowball fights or light the barbeque. Animals may be associated with particular seasons by what they do, for example, some hibernate, some change their feathers and some form chrysalises. Finally, the children can then write their opinion of that season.

If you want to, you could give the children sentence starter prompts such as:

- Autumn is...
- It is...
- The weather is...
- It makes you...
- The animals are...

Teaching tip

Encourage the children to add adjectives, verbs and adverbs to their poem at every line. They could even add similes on every other line to extend the imagery.

IDEA 18

First World War poetry

'These men are worth your tears.' (Wilfred Owen, *Apologia Pro Poemate Meo*)

Children create onomatopoeia poetry based on Wilfred Owen's First World War poems.

Teaching tip

There is a fantastic reading of 'Dulce et Decorum Est' by Christopher Eccleston on YouTube.

Taking it further

The children could then go on to write their own free verse including more onomatopoeia. They could choose their subject matter and compare these to the First World War poems.

As mentioned earlier, onomatopoeia is a type of figurative language where the word means the sound it makes. 'Splash', 'mumble', 'gargle', 'slam', 'bash', 'eek' and 'argh' are all examples of this.

Wilfred Owen was a poet who used this form of figurative language to great effect. He chronicled his experiences of the First World War through his poetry. In his poem 'Dulce et Decorum Est', the title is taken from a line by the Roman poet Horace, which means, 'It is sweet and fitting to die for one's country.' Here are some examples of lines in the poem that use onomatopoeia (shown in bold):

***coughing** like hags*
*deaf even to the **hoots***
*He plunges at me, **guttering, choking***
*Come **gargling** from the froth-corrupted lungs*

Ask the children to make word banks of onomatopoeia words taken from 'Dulce et Decorum Est' or other poems by Wilfred Owen. They can then write their own poems using Owen's as inspiration. For example, their poems could use the lines above but make changes to the language (yet keeping the same onomatopoeia). For example:

Coughing constantly
Loud and deafening hoots all around
He falls upon me guttering, choking
Gargling blood and spitting death

Viking kennings

'In *Beowulf*, "battle-sweat" means blood.'

Children label a Viking warrior's weapons and armour using kennings (noun and verb combinations). They use kennings to write riddles too.

Kennings are two-word phrases originating in Old Norse poetry. The Anglo-Saxon poem *Beowulf* uses many kennings, for example, a body is described as a 'bone-house' and a sword is a 'battle-light'. An easy way to write kennings is to join a noun to a verb with a hyphen. For example, eyes could be 'food-finders' or fingers could be 'pencil-holders'.

To keep with the Norse theme, you could show an image of a Viking warrior to the children. They could then write noun labels for the weapons and armour, such as 'helmet', 'mail armour', 'sword', 'bearded axe' and 'shield'.

Kennings can then be written to describe each of these labels. For example, the helmet could be a 'head-protector', the sword could be a 'head-chopper', the bearded axe could be a 'king-killer', and the shield could be a 'bone-breaker'. These can then be written up as a poem to describe a Viking warrior.

Kennings can also be used as riddles, so that children have to guess what is being described with the kennings. For example:

Silent-stalker
Chicken-eater
Night-hunter
Stealthy-prowler

This poem describes a fox. Ask the children to choose an animal and write a poem about it just using kennings. They can then try to guess which animals are being described.

Taking it further

You could give the children pictures of animals and ask them to label each part of each animal with kennings.

IDEA 20

Zombie haikus

'Five syllables here, seven more syllables here, are you happy now?'

Children write haikus to describe a zombie apocalypse, using a syllable pattern of five for the first line, seven for the second line and five for the third line.

Haikus are a form of Japanese poetry made up of three lines. The first and last lines have five syllables each and the middle line has seven syllables, making a total of 17 syllables. Search online for John Cooper Clarke's famous haiku, which shows how keeping to the 17-syllable limit is very 'diffic' indeed!

There are numerous examples of haikus online about a wide range of subjects. Ryan Mecum has written books of vampire, werewolf and zombie haikus. In an interview about his book *Zombie Haiku*, Mecum said, 'I liked the idea of a zombie poet who kept a haiku journal of his journey... I tried to take the more stereotypical zombie clichés, but then tried writing about them from different angles than the norm.'

Ask the children to write their own zombie haikus about coping in a zombie apocalypse. There could be five verses and each verse could have a different theme, for example: describing a zombie; describing what they can find for a weapon; battling with a zombie; making a location safe; and a cliffhanger ending.

Teaching tip

Zombies don't have to be the theme. You could choose anything and ask the children to use the haiku structure to write about topics such as animals, seasons or a sport.

Bonus idea ★

Use haikus as greetings in cards for Christmas, Diwali, Valentine's Day or other such festivals and special days.

Mecum, R. (2008), *Zombie Haiku: Good Poetry For Your... Brains*. Cincinnatti, OH: HOW Books.

Character

Heraldry

'You're such a knight in shining armour!'

Children describe themselves by choosing heraldic colours and symbols after discovering their meaning.

Taking it further

Explore other heraldic symbolism by going to the website www.heraldryandcrests.com/pages/heraldic-symbolism-a-z. The children can then add detail to their own heraldic crests by choosing more features, objects, colours or lines.

During the Middle Ages, there were ten main heraldic colours that reflected the personalities of the knights who wore them on their tabards, flags and shields. Red represented strength, white meant peaceful, blue was for loyalty and friendship, yellow or gold was for kindness and generosity, green was for being hopeful, orange was for wanting to be the best, brown was for a winner, purple meant you believed in justice, pink meant you believed in love, and black meant you were sad.

The images, which were often of animals, carried meaning too. An image of a dragon meant you were courageous. There are numerous examples online, but here are some examples:

Horse = always ready.	Dog = loyal.
Rabbit = peace loving.	Snake = clever.
Deer = skilful.	Wild boar = fierce.
Unicorn = good at writing poetry.	Lion = strong.

The children could choose a heraldic design to show the personality of a character. If their knight wears a red and white tabard, then their character doesn't like to fight as they are peaceful, but if forced can certainly win a battle as they are strong. If their character has the symbol of a unicorn on their chest then they might recite the odd poem or two. Once the children have chosen a heraldic design they can write character descriptions of knights such as, 'She has a horse painted on her shield to show that she is always ready for battle.'

Willy Wonka

'If you want to view paradise, simply look around and view it.' (Willy Wonka in *Willy Wonka & The Chocolate Factory,* film)

Children explore the Oompa-Loompas' opinions of Willy Wonka from Roald Dahl's *Charlie and the Chocolate Factory*. Is Willy Wonka kind and eccentric or an evil slave master?

Most children would consider Willy Wonka to be a good character. If you asked children to describe him then they might use adjectives such as 'nice', 'good' and 'kind'. We might ask children to justify their answers with examples from the text, and they might say that he is 'good' because he teaches Charlie the secrets of his factory.

However, we can present children with an alternative view and challenge their perspectives by giving other examples in the text. He is a character that can be insensitive, uncaring and judgemental.

For example, what about the treatment of the Oompa-Loompas? On the one hand, Willy Wonka is their saviour who has rescued them from Loompaland. Willy Wonka saves them by taking them to his factory where they get their most favourite food: chocolate!

On the other hand, Willy Wonka could be compared to a slave master. He has taken the Oompa-Loompas from their home and made them work in his factory for beans!

By presenting well-known characters in alternative ways to children, we are challenging their learning. When children feel passionate about something and want to make their opinion known then this is reflected in their writing. For example, could they write a character description of Harry Potter focusing on the events that led to Cedric Diggory's demise?

Teaching tip

You could also use the example of Violet Beauregarde. When Violet inflates, Willy Wonka is not in the least bit remorseful or concerned for her wellbeing.

Taking it further

Use other famous characters from books and challenge the children's opinions about them. Is the Gruffalo good or bad and why? What about Peter Pan?

Design a robot friend

'Danger, Will Robinson!' (Robot B9 in the TV show *Lost in Space*)

Using the TV advert for the robot 'Jibo' as a stimulus, children design a robot character to be their companion.

Jibo is a social robot with artificial intelligence which didn't quite make the market. The advert for Jibo on YouTube shows the robot interacting with a family in a variety of ways, including taking pictures, reminding them of appointments, telling a story and ordering takeaway food.

However, Jibo never quite made it out of America as other virtual assistant technologies were smaller, cheaper and could do a lot more.

The advert for Jibo though has great potential for children. They could design a second-generation Jibo: Jibo2! This Jibo can do anything they want it to. Ask the children to design what Jibo2 will look like. It could perhaps have the same smooth aluminium shell but be given upgrades such as arms, legs and hands. They could then explore how Jibo2 would move around. There could be wheels or even a jet pack.

Jibo was originally wired with a plug for power, but Jibo2 could be powered by anything: water, sunlight or fairy dust. Jibo2 might also be able to do homework, tidy bedrooms, make pizza, teach dance moves... the only limit is how far children's imaginations can take them in their writing.

Teaching tip

When discussing what could power the robot, watch the animation 'Powerless - a modern day Pinocchio' from the Literacy Shed website.

Bonus idea ★

Ask the children to take this work home and show their family. They could then design a family robot as a homework activity.

Zombies

'Braaaaaaaaiiiiiiiiiinnnnnnnnnssssss!'

Children use portrait techniques to draw a zombie face and then describe it using rich vocabulary.

Ask the children to draw portraits, starting by drawing an oval shape for the head. Then ask the children to look at each other to help with proportions and sizes. Ask the children to notice that the eyes and ears are level with each other and are situated right in the centre of the head. Necks are not as wide as the head but are still thick, and shoulders go out way past the head. Hair doesn't just grow right on the top of the head but rather comes down towards the forehead.

Ask the children to draw portraits based on these observations onto the oval shapes already drawn. These portraits are not meant to be pictures of their friends, but rather a generic portrait.

Then ask the children to give these portraits a 'zombie twist' by adding a green-grey skin tone. They can extend the jaw, add horrible teeth and draw lines under the eyes.

Once the portraits are complete, the children can choose adjectives such as 'scary', 'threatening' and 'disgusting', and verbs such as 'moaning', 'growled' and 'staring'. You could use the 'Characters' section in Alison Wilcox's *Descriptosaurus* to suggest adjectives such as 'demon-haunted', 'malicious' and 'callous', and verbs such as 'rasping', 'darkened' and 'glinted'. The children can also walk around the classroom to look at the vocabulary choices made by others and 'magpie' some of these words for their own portraits.

Taking it further

This same technique can be adapted to create fairy portraits, mermaid portraits, pirate portraits, Stone Age portraits and any other types that you can think of.

IDEA 25

Superheroes

'Is it a bird? Is it a plane? No, it's Superman!'

Children choose which superpower they would most want. They then describe their superhero name, costume, sidekick and vehicle.

Teaching tip

Superhero names often involve alliteration or rhyme, which you could ask the children to include in their own superhero names.

Taking it further

Villains could be created and narrative stories planned about how the superheroes defeat the villains and save the world. Further adventures could be added involving other villains, natural disasters or origin stories as to how the superheroes got their powers.

Superheroes are vast and varied. Spiderman has the abilities of a super spider, Aquaman can talk to fish and Superman can fly and shoot laser beams from his eyeballs.

Ask the children which superpower they would most want, such as invisibility, telekinesis (the ability to use your mind to move objects), fire powers or speed. Their power might be reflected in their chosen superhero name, such as The Invisible Girl, Magic Mind, Flame Dude or Bolt Boy.

Children could then design and describe a suit or costume. Batman and Iron Man don't actually have powers and rely entirely on their suits. Superheroes often have gadgets in utility belts. Sometimes they have an object which also gives them powers, like Thor's hammer.

Some superheroes have sidekicks, like Batman's Robin. These sidekicks can sometimes be animals with powers, such as a talking dog or super-intelligent racoon. The children could design and describe their own animal sidekick.

Finally, the children could design vehicles like Batman's Batcycle or Wonder Woman's invisible plane. It could be rocket boots, a speed boat, a racing car or anything else they can think of.

The children can then write a detailed description of their superhero in the first person.

Stereotypes

'Yes I can!'

Children break stereotypical ideas about disabled people using Channel 4's 'We're the Superhumans' TV advert for the 2016 Paralympics.

The Paralympics have been celebrating sport for athletes with impairments since 1960.

Books such as R. J. Palacio's *Wonder* have done great things for raising awareness, understanding and tolerance towards all people too. You could show the children a picture of Auggie and many of them would recognise him from *Wonder*: the book or the film. You could ask the children how they would treat Auggie if he started at their school, and it is likely that their answers would be filled with kindness towards a new friend.

You could also show the children pictures of people with some sort of impairment and ask what things they may or may not be able to do. After this, show them Channel 4's 'We're the Superhumans' TV advert for the 2016 Paralympics. It shows incredible athletes doing the most astonishing things.

After viewing the advert, ask the children to review their original answers about what people with impairments can and cannot do. They could then write a character description about a person with an impairment and describe all of the amazing things they do. Adverbs such as 'determinedly', 'relentlessly', 'persistently', 'resolutely', 'heroically', 'untiringly' and 'single-mindedly' could be offered on the board as prompts.

Teaching tip

R. J. Palacio's *Wonder* shows the prejudice and discrimination that some people face, and also shows the resilience it takes to overcome this. This can lead to an excellent class discussion and PSHE lessons to take this further.

IDEA 27

Letters from the Front

'In your last letter you asked me to let you know something of what I have gone through...'

Children write First World War letters, revealing a person's character through what is and isn't included.

One Boy's War by Lynn Huggins-Cooper tells the tale of Sydney who, despite being underage, signs up to fight in the First World War. He is posted to Ypres and the horrors of the trenches are revealed almost immediately. It is a touching and tragic true story. One part includes a letter from Sydney to his mother. He tells her that he is having a good time, eating bully-beef every day and that he will be home for Christmas. None of which is true.

Ask the children why he didn't mention the soupy trench water, the rats the size of cats and the lice-infested uniforms. Or why he didn't describe the constant sounds of the shells, the freezing conditions and the friends being killed all around.

On the Imperial War Museums' website there is a section entitled 'Letters to Loved Ones'. These include a letter from a woman to her fiancé in the trenches, and a child's letter to his father. They are moving and informative. It is often what is *not* being said that reveals more about the writer of the letter than what *is* being said.

This can lead to a mature classroom discussion on being selfless, and devoting care and attention when writing letters. Ask the children to either write a letter from the Front or a reply from home. They should consider which 'white lies' will be included, what will be left out and what sort of language and tone they should use.

Teaching tip

The National Archives website also offers lots of examples of real letters that can be shared and discussed with the children.

Taking it further

Ask the children to write setting descriptions of the trenches using their five senses, based on the real letters that you have shared with them.

Figurative language

'You don't know the difference between literally and figuratively, do you?' (Klaus Baudelaire in A *Series of Unfortunate Events* by Lemony Snicket)

Children use an extract from *A Series of Unfortunate Events* to explain and use metaphor, similes and hyperbole.

In Lemony Snicket's *A Series of Unfortunate Events: The Bad Beginning*, the narrator, Snicket himself, says: 'If something happens literally, it actually happens; if something happens figuratively, it feels like it is happening.' He uses the phrase 'jumping for joy' as an example; you can find a clip of it on YouTube. It's a perfect way of showing the difference between something that actually happens and something that we are merely describing in a particular way.

Children can overuse similes in their writing, so it's important we teach other forms of figurative language from a young age. For example, children can upgrade their similes with hyperbole. They might change a simile such as 'she was as kind as a friend giving you a gift' to 'she was more generous than Father Christmas standing on your doorstep every day lavishing you with every gift you ever wanted.'

Hyperbole can also be applied to metaphor. For example, they could change 'she was a nightmare' to 'she was a venomous nightmare sent from the deepest, darkest pit that ever existed'.

The children could be given literal sentences such as 'he was tall' and they could then write figurative descriptions to expand these sentences, such as 'he was as tall as the Eiffel Tower being lifted into the sky by a giant'.

Teaching tip

When using any form of figurative language, repetition is to be avoided at all costs. Sentences that contain too many metaphors or similes lead to bad writing. When using alliteration this is also the case. For example, 'a wild wind whipped the weather-worn faces of the withered witches' is far too much alliteration. A general rule is to include no more than three same sounds in a sentence.

Character through dialogue

'Your deeds are your monuments.' (*Wonder* by R. J. Palacio)

Children look at how actions reveal a person's character, by examining fictional heroes and using dialogue to say what they have done.

'He is the greatest hero that has ever been!' declared the Queen, 'He has saved every soul in the palace from the fire!'

Without describing the specific events in detail, we know from these descriptions that someone has done a great deal to earn the respect of a queen. What other people say about heroes can reveal something about their character.

Ask the children to choose five people, such as a king, princess, duke, villager and mother. Each of these people should then say something about a hero which reveals something of that hero's character. For example, 'Wow! Did you see how she...' or 'Did you know, he single-handedly...'.

This can work as an introduction to a particular hero character study. But remember that heroes in stories are not always portrayed in a positive way. For example, Theseus, who slayed the Minotaur, left Princess Ariadne on an island to starve to death. So perhaps the actions performed by a hero are overshadowed by other choices they make. Ask children to reveal flaws in character through dialogue. For example, 'Theseus killed the Minotaur, but did you hear what he did to poor Ariadne?'

Taking it further

Ask the children to choose their favourite character from a book, TV show or film. Ask them to imagine going to a party where this person will be arriving shortly. Everyone there knows this character really well. The children should write what people say about this character before they arrive.

Animal transformations

'I have a class of animals!'

Children describe the process of turning into an animal by focusing on each body part, step by step.

Begin by showing the children the 2016 Rio Olympics advert from the BBC. It shows rainforest animals taking part in Olympic sports. There is a gymnast sloth, synchronised swimming crocodiles, a hammer-throwing anteater and more. At the end of the advert the animals become human.

Ask the children to imagine themselves turning into an animal. Ask them to close their eyes and picture what would happen to their ears first. Would these become bigger or smaller or even just fall off? Would their skin grow fur, feathers or scales? Does their skin change colour, texture or shape? What would happen to their eyes, nose and hair?

Show the children a small section of the animated film *Blackface*. Begin at three minutes into the film. It shows a hunter turning into a monkey. First, his ears grow larger, then he drops his gun as his hands change shape. His skin grows hair and he begins to shrink. Eventually, he climbs out of his clothes and is a monkey.

Give the children sentence starter prompts with time conjunctions, such as 'First of all my ears began to...', 'Then, my eyes...' or 'Next, my skin was...'.

Teaching tip

It's important that the children don't tell each other their chosen animal. Once completed, the children could then read their descriptions to each other and try to guess the animals they have turned into. Or children could take turns reading out their descriptions and the person who guesses correctly could read theirs next.

Persuasion

IDEA 31

Muhammad Ali boasting

'Float like a butterfly, sting like a bee.' (Muhammad Ali)

Children convince others of their own greatness by describing themselves using Muhammad Ali's 'Rumble in the Jungle' poem as a template.

'Rumble in the Jungle' is a poem that Muhammad Ali performed before his match with George Foreman in 1974. It starts like this:

Last night I had a dream, When I got to Africa,
I had one hell of a rumble.
I had to beat Tarzan's behind first,
For claiming to be King of the Jungle.
For this fight, I've wrestled with alligators,
I've tussled with a whale.

There are a variety of clips on YouTube showing Ali performing this now famous poem. They show all the energy and passion that Ali possessed, and can be a great inspiration for children to write their own version. You could give the children a template, including lines such as:

Last night I had a dream, when I got to ________,
I had a crazy rumble, I had to beat ________.
I handcuffed lightning, I've ________ a whale.
I've ________ and thrown thunder in jail.
I'm so mean, I make ________ sick.
I'm so fast, I can ________ and don't get wet.
I can run through ________ or ________ and it's no threat.

Teaching tip

This is heavily scaffolded so perhaps you could adapt this for your class by taking out some of the rhymes at the end of the lines, or some of the verbs such as 'handcuffed', 'thrown' or 'run'. These could be replaced with alternatives or the children could simply write their own poems that boast of impossible things: things that might persuade others to form an opinion of great fear or tremendous admiration.

Slay the dragon... please!

'Good manners cost nothing.'

Children write a persuasive letter to a king or queen, persuading them to send a hero to defeat a dragon.

Set the scene that a ferocious and deadly dragon has been destroying villages and towns in a fictitious land. Explain to the children that they are to imagine they live in this land. They must write a letter to the royal family to request they send a hero to defeat the dragon.

To plan this letter, the children should first create some vocabulary to describe the dragon. This could include expanded noun phrases with adjectives, such as 'huge, terrifying and destructive claws'. Children could also add verbs and adverbs to describe what the dragon has been doing, such as 'rapidly chasing', 'hungrily devouring' or 'constantly destroying'.

Children could then go on to make up a royal name, such as Queen Snodgrass or King Hacking Bottom. An imaginary hero could then be created, as well as lists of his or her previous deeds (such as rescuing a unicorn from an army of ogres or saving a blobfish from the kraken).

Once all of these parts of the imaginary scenario are in place, the children can use their knowledge of persuasive letter-writing to write a letter explaining why the dragon needs to be defeated and why this hero is the best person for the job. Conjunctions that persuade, the urgency of the present tense, a range of persuasive arguments with supporting evidence, opening statements, a summary and a conclusion can all be included.

Taking it further

A fictitious palace address could also be created, such as:

- Diamond Palace on the Hill
- Golden Town, MO99 NEY
- Castle Fairytale in the Clouds, Far Far Away, FA1 1RY.

Bonus idea ★

You could ask the children to write a reply from the king or queen. The response could outline the reasons why they are willing or not willing to send any help. Factors such as money, distance and availability may influence the response.

IDEA 33

I have a dream

'I have a dream that one day this nation will rise up and live out the true meaning of its creed: "We hold these truths to be self-evident, that all men are created equal."' (Martin Luther King Jr.)

Children explore the children's hopes and dreams for the world using Martin Luther King's famous speech for inspiration.

Martin Luther King's speech 'I Have a Dream', delivered on 28 August 1963 as part of the March on Washington for Jobs and Freedom, is just as inspirational to listen to today as it was back then. There are clips available to watch online as well as explanatory documentaries for children. You could begin by watching the speech or exploring further resources about the meaning in the speech.

After this, ask the children to say what they dream to change in the world. You could give examples of stopping world hunger, ending homelessness or curing cancer. But perhaps the best examples would be given by the children themselves. Allow them to talk to each other about what is important to them.

Using these discussions as a stimulus, the children could write their own 'I Have a Dream' speech. You could give them a structure to follow, such as:

> *I have a dream today. I have a dream that one day...*
> *I have a dream today. I have a dream that one day...*
> *I have a dream today. I have a dream that one day...*
> *I have a dream.*

This way they could explore three themes to change the world. Or you could adapt this for a single change or multiple changes.

Taking it further

These hopes and dreams could be shared in the classroom, across the whole school in an assembly or even further afield such as by being posted to a local politician. They could even be sent to Downing Street or posted online for a global audience.

Can I keep it?

'A dog is for life, not just for Christmas. But a monster?'

Children design a mythical monster and write a persuasive letter to the headteacher outlining the reasons why it should be kept as a pet in the school.

Ask the children to imagine finding an egg in the school grounds. You could even hide one that the children could discover. It could be big or small, spotted or striped, glowing or camouflaged. The children could then design a creature that lives inside the egg. It might have horns, a snout or a beak. It could be feathered, scaly or smooth. It might have multiple legs, arms or heads. Perhaps it has extraordinary abilities such as teleportation, breathing fire or being able to turn invisible.

If the creature was to live in the school grounds, the children might have to design a special enclosure to meet its needs: food, drink and somewhere to sleep. It may also need some form of entertainment like a pool or hot tub, and perhaps a safety barrier too.

The children should then think about the benefits such a creature could have on school life. How could it help the children, teachers and dinner staff? Are there any negative aspects to having the creature live at school and how can these be addressed?

Now the children should have gathered enough information to write a structured letter to their headteacher, persuading them to keep the monster at school. This should include all of the planned elements: what the creature looks like, what its needs are, what the positive and negative elements are for having such a creature on site, and finally, how all of these might benefit the school.

Teaching tip

The children could try using emotive language such as 'Surely you would not...', 'After all, it was found right here...' or 'It is our duty to look after...'

Taking it further

The children may also need to think about what happens when the creature grows. Does it evolve in some way? Does its size or do its powers change?

IDEA 35

Propaganda

'Keep Calm... It's The Weekend!'

Children examine the propaganda posters of the First and Second World Wars. Children then design their own versions in the same style.

The phrase 'Keep Calm and Carry On' has become familiar to all of us through being used in advertising campaigns, on T-shirts, in greetings cards and many more places besides. Variations can even be seen in the staff room, with 'Keep Calm and Teach' on mugs, 'Keep Calm and Press Control-Alt-Delete' on posters above computers and 'Keep Calm and Wash Your Dishes Please!' above the sink. During SATs week, 'Keep Calm and Smash Your SATs', 'Keep Calm, It's Only SATs', or 'Keep Calm and Good Luck in Your SATs' decorate the walls of some schools.

Teaching tip

In propaganda posters, colour is important. Children should look at the examples and consider whether to use bold colours, dark colours or pastel shades for their own posters.

Taking it further

Children could also consider how the Union Jack is used for persuasion. Could the children include a flag in their own posters? How and why is this effective in persuasion?

The origin of the phrase may be unfamiliar to some children. During the Second World War, posters which contained motivational words were used to raise the morale of Britain. 'Keep Calm and Carry On' was just one of these posters, released by the British government in 1939 during the threat of mass air raids. Other posters such as 'Come Into The Factories', 'Help Britain Finish the Job!' and 'They Can't Get on Without Us' were plastered over the streets.

The images used to accompany the slogans were equally as important. 'Come Into the Factories' shows a uniformed woman with her arms held aloft outside a factory, commanding a squadron of planes to take to the skies. The implication is that those who work in the factories are playing an equally important role to those fighting on the front line. Thus, it is necessary that those still at home should

'Come Into the Factories' to do their duty for Britain and help a country at war.

Look at other First and Second World War propaganda posters from Britain and other countries. Sometimes the slogans may be ambiguous and need explaining, such as 'Loose Lips Sink Ships', 'Keep Mum – She's Not So Dumb' or 'Keep a Pig – Join or Start a Pig Club'. Ask the children to discuss the phrases and look for common patterns such as rhyme or alliteration, as in 'Lend a Hand on the Land' or 'Fighting Fit in the Factory'.

Then look at the images used to accompany the words. Are there common themes or colours? How are animals used to portray emotion? It could be discussed as to why a lion is used so frequently in the British posters and an eagle in the American ones.

The children could then select a persuasive theme linked to the First or Second World War, such as persuading people to sign up to fight, to work in the factories, to grow their own food, to not gossip with others about the war or to leave the city for the safety of the countryside.

Children could then create their own memorable and persuasive slogans using rhyme, alliteration or figurative language such as simile, onomatopoeia or personification. They could then consider what images could accompany their slogans to make them more powerful. They could perhaps use a person, people or an animal.

Bonus idea ★

Animals feature heavily in propaganda posters. The children can explore which animals feature most frequently and why. They could then consider which animal they would choose to create a persuasive poster for school on picking up litter or choosing a school dinner over a packed lunch, and so on.

IDEA 36

Afternoon playtime

'Afternoon playtimes are more trouble than they're worth.'

Children discuss and then write about the pros and cons of afternoon playtime, writing a balanced argument that reflects conflicting opinions, finishing with a conclusion.

Some schools recommend an afternoon playtime while others do not. Some have replaced afternoon playtimes with exercise activities such as 'the daily mile'. There are children who prefer not to go outside too, especially during winter. Some volunteer in the school library, some request 'jobs' from their teacher to do in the classroom, and others volunteer to help in younger classrooms.

In 2019, the *Guardian* ran an article about the impact that losing afternoon playtime has on children's abilities to develop their social skills and make friends. They also argued that these playtimes are essential for children's wellbeing and development. In most schools, the issue of afternoon playtimes will lead to divided opinions. Children might consider that if they did not have an afternoon playtime then perhaps the school day could be shorter or lunchtime could be longer.

Sometimes children can argue with each other after partaking in sporting activities such as football during break times. As a result, lesson time after breaks can be reduced as time is taken to solve these issues. This means that lesson time can be lost.

Once a variety of pros and cons have been discussed with the class as a whole, the children could further explore their own opinions with friends, either in partners or

Teaching tip

Simpler sentence starter prompts could be used for younger children such as 'It is important that...', 'Let us remember...' and 'I think...'

small groups. During this time, sentence starter prompts could be given such as:

There are a number of reasons as to why...
Surely, childhood is so precious that...
Most teachers would agree that...
Furthermore, experts state...
Surely children would learn more by...
In conclusion, if...

These can be adapted and differentiated according to the age and ability of the children in your class, but the general theme can still be used. Children could choose from your sentence starters or make up ones of their own, continuing them to write persuasive sentences such as:

There are a number of reasons as to why schools should not have an afternoon playtime, such as disturbing exciting lessons in the classroom like science or art.
Surely, childhood is so precious that it should not be spent indoors.
Most teachers would agree that afternoon playtimes cause problems that have to be dealt with in the classroom.
Furthermore, experts state it helps children to make friends.
Surely, children would learn more by having longer lessons in the afternoon like history, music, or design and technology.
In conclusion, if afternoon playtimes were banned then children will lose valuable exercise time but gain more learning time in the classroom.

These sentences could then be shared and discussed in class, before going on to write a balanced argument representing both opinions. However, the children should then draw a conclusion that firmly supports one viewpoint and seeks to persuade others to reach the same opinion.

Taking it further

The children could use this template to create a balanced argument relating to a different topic, such as healthy eating versus takeaway food, or attending school versus home schooling.

IDEA 37

Superheroes are good... aren't they?

'You either die a hero or live long enough to see yourself become the villain.' (Harvey Dent in *The Dark Knight*)

Children look at the fight scene between Batman and Superman. They choose a side and explain why they are rooting for that particular hero. This leads to writing a persuasive argument for why one superhero is better than all the others.

In the film *Batman v Superman: Dawn of Justice*, the fight scenes between the two superheroes involve a lot of wreckage. In one scene, walls are knocked down, staircases wrecked and a building destroyed. You can show the children a scene from the film or from a more suitable cartoon version on YouTube. Ask the children who their favourite is – Batman or Superman – then ask them to tell each other why. Ask the children why the two superheroes are fighting each other. Why would good characters ever want to fight?

Next, ask the children to choose any favourite superhero. It could be Spider-Gwen, Marshall from *Paw Patrol* or Thor. Any superhero will do. Then ask them to imagine their superhero having to battle another superhero, as Batman and Superman did. There could be Peppa Pig v Wolverine battles, or Luna Girl from *PJ Masks* could battle Star-Lord from *Guardians of the Galaxy*. The children have to explain why they want their favourite superhero to win. Why is their chosen superhero better than all of the rest?

The children can then present a persuasive argument that outlines why their superhero is not just better than any supervillain, but also better than any other superhero, giving reasons to justify their opinions.

Taking it further

The persuasive argument could be written into bullet points and presented as a poster, as part of a campaign to get the superhero elected into a position of authority. There could be posters with titles such as 'Iron Man for president because...' or 'Wonder Woman should be the new prime minister because...'

When wishes go wrong

'You'll never have a friend like me!' (The Genie in *Aladdin*)

Children discuss genies and their wish-giving abilities, then explore which three wishes they would ask for. What happens if the language used is too ambiguous and the genie misunderstands what it is you actually want?

In Arabian mythology, genies feature in stories such as 'Aladdin' and 'The Epic of Gilgamesh'. Such genies are not always good characters; some are tricksters who've been trapped and promise wishes for their release.

Ask the children what they would wish for if they found a genie's lamp. The children can write or draw as many wishes as they want onto whiteboards and compare these to their friends' wishes. They must then select their favourite three and wipe off the rest.

Explain that if the children are not absolutely clear in what they ask for then their wishes can go wrong. For example, if they wish for a million pounds then this might come falling from the sky and squash them. Or if they wish to be the world's greatest ballerina, they might have to go on an endless world tour and never see their family and friends again. A wish for limitless supplies of chocolate might give them a type of chocolate that they don't like.

Explain that you are going to pretend to be the genie. The children must persuade you to grant their wishes in the correct way, as they would actually like them to be fulfilled, by using specific and accurate language. It is only through this precision that you will be persuaded to grant the wishes.

The children then write their wishes and present them to you for your genie judgement.

Teaching tip

You can watch clips from Disney's *Aladdin* and the new action film on YouTube. These include scenes where the genie explains the three rules of wish-making.

Bonus idea ★

Children could put a sticky note on the board with a wish on it. The children then use a different-coloured sticky note to say why it would be a good wish, or an alternative colour to say why the wish wouldn't work.

Is graffiti art?

'Art is no crime... it is every artist's responsibility to make art that is meaningful.' (Shirin Neshat)

Children look at famous graffiti artists such as Banksy and Lady Pink, then compare this art style to other examples of street graffiti. What makes one type art and the other vandalism? This leads to writing a persuasive argument about whether graffiti is or isn't art.

Graffiti murals by Bansky such as *Girl with Balloon*, *Slave Labour* and *Bomb Hugger* have become accepted as works of art. Some Banksy murals have been removed and sold at auction, fetching huge prices. But what makes these murals worth so much when other works of graffiti are considered to be such an eyesore?

Show the children a range of graffiti including murals, tags, wildstyle, stencils, paste-up posters and slap stickers. Ask them what they think of each type. Ask them if they would like any of these examples either inside or outside their homes, and ask them to give reasons for this.

Explain that some people think that graffiti is art as it allows artists to express themselves in their own creative way. But others think that it is vandalism rather than art, as it involves painting or decorating public spaces that the artists have not been given permission to paint on. Ask the children to discuss and research other opinions on websites, YouTube, books and with each other. They could then write a persuasive argument as to why graffiti is or isn't art with their own opinions given throughout.

Taking it further

The children's opinions could be summarised further into a phrase and slogan. These could then be 'graffitied' onto a display board.

Bonus idea ★

The children could try to summarise their opinion in a tweet (which can only have up to 280 characters in it). They should use all 280 characters including spaces between words, but not exceed the limit.

Zoos or prisons?

'Animals shouldn't be kept in cages. It's cruel.'

Children examine the pros and cons of zoos. They then write a persuasive argument giving their opinion.

There are over ten thousand zoos in the world, but only around 240 are part of the Association of Zoos and Aquariums (AZA). The zoos that are part of the AZA are regulated to ensure the rights of the animals are protected, and that they live in healthy and safe environments. Responsible breeding programmes are also followed in AZA zoos.

Dr Dave Hone wrote an article in the *Guardian* in 2014 that outlined 'Why Zoos Are Good'. However, in the same year, Hannah Barnes from the BBC ran an article on 'How Many Healthy Animals Do Zoos Put Down?'

Begin by looking at websites such as www.animal-ethics.org or www.nationalgeographic.com. On these there are many arguments for and against zoos.

After exploring these websites and other sources of information, ask the children to do their own research into zoos and aquariums, perhaps for homework or at school. A list of child-friendly websites could be offered to families to support this activity. Or perhaps this could be a 'talk homework' where children simply discuss what they have been doing at school with their families.

Once a knowledge base has been established and children have formed their own opinions, then the question 'Are zoos prisons?' can be asked. The children should write their own persuasive arguments, outlining their opinions and giving clear reasons for them.

Taking it further

These persuasive arguments could form the starting point for a classroom debate, which could be showcased to the rest of the school in an assembly. At the end, the whole school could vote for which side of the argument they agree with once they have heard the opposing views.

Bonus idea ★

Have a look at the www.petakids.com website (specifically for the under 12s) with quizzes, videos, photos, games, comics and activities.

Narrative

Mini sagas

'Many children in my class think that writing has to be lengthy to be good. I want them to understand the importance of being concise and using language carefully and precisely.'

An important and sometimes neglected skill in writing is being concise. For most publications (including this one!) there are word limits that have to be adhered to. This activity requires writers to tell a story in exactly 50 words.

Show children some examples of 'mini sagas': short stories consisting of exactly 50 words. You can find plenty of these in books or online (see, for example, the website www.fiftywordstories.com), or you could write your own.

Ask the children to help you write a 50-word version of a well-known story, such as *Goldilocks and the Three Bears*. To begin with, don't count the words but display the story on the board, before asking children to help you reduce the word count by taking out unnecessary words and details. Read and reread the story and ask if anything significant is missing.

This activity lends itself to paired work because it's important for children to discuss not only the stories they write but also the way they are phrased and the vocabulary used.

Encourage children to plan their own mini sagas by making notes of key events, and then ask them to draft, edit and revise until they are happy they have produced a good 50-word version. Read these aloud and ask for feedback from the rest of the class.

Teaching tip

Model concise writing with children before asking them to work independently or in pairs. Show how some words (such as 'got') are often superfluous, and how some phrases can be written more concisely (for example, 'in spite of the fact that' could become 'despite'.

Taking it further

You might go on to get children to produce the stories as Word files, and create a class book of mini sagas or a wall display with pictures included.

Six-word stories

'I want an activity in which every child can achieve something in writing.'

Children write stories that are only six words long. These are a good starting point for longer writing, but they also show how very short pieces can be powerful and full of meaning.

'For sale: baby shoes, never worn.' This six-word story is an example of a piece of 'flash fiction', often attributed to the writer Ernest Hemingway.

Tell the children that you've written a story and it's only six words long. Share your example and challenge the children to think of others. Let them try writing these on mini whiteboards or tablets, and ask them to share what they've done with neighbours and then with the rest of the class. The children could do this by retelling a complete story as briefly as they can and then work on reducing it further into only six words. Perhaps they could even practise by describing a lesson in six words, a lunchtime in six words or their family in six words.

Write some of their examples on the board and discuss them. Then ask children to produce more six-word stories independently or in pairs. Discuss and display the results.

Teaching tip

Find examples suitable for sharing with children and write some of your own. These can be poignant or amusing. Try www.sixwordstories.net and www.thewritepractice.com/six-word.

Taking it further

A possible development is to use six-word stories in other areas of the curriculum. For example, children might retell a historical event in six words or sum up a science experiment. You might develop this further by introducing other word limit targets for brief pieces of writing.

IDEA 43

Story openings

'Now that most of my class are reading more sophisticated texts, I'd like them to think about the features of good narrative writing.'

Children look at literature to consider what makes a good story opening that might encourage them to read on.

Teaching tip

Look through books in the class library and make a collection of story openings to show to the children. Display these and ask children to rate them on a 1-to-10 scale according to how well they feel the openings engage their interest.

Taking it further

This activity can be the catalyst for extended writing, but it is equally valid to move on after focusing only on story openings.

Read and show some examples of story openings to the children and ask them for their views. What do they like and dislike? Which ones make them want to read on? Discuss the importance of grabbing the reader's attention right from the start of a story, and share some examples which 'start with a bang'. For example, you could use Iain Banks' *The Crow Road* which begins, 'It was the day my grandmother exploded.'

Show the children a range of opening sentences from books that start with an exciting sentence such as 'It was a bright, cold day in April and the clocks were striking thirteen' from George Orwell's *1984* or 'All children grow up, except one' from J. M. Barrie's *Peter Pan*.

Ask the children to write their own sentence for a story opening, and explain that these will be displayed somehow (perhaps by being made into a class book or put on the school website so that others can read them). Encourage the children to read each other's work and to make suggestions.

Ask the children to read their openings to groups who can suggest what might happen next. They might go on to take each other's openings and write the next paragraph before handing it back and asking the original author to revise it and continue the story.

Story endings

'I want to encourage my class to consider more carefully ways of ending their stories.'

While providing story openings as a stimulus for writing is quite common, we rarely use story endings in the same way. Find examples of final sentences for children to analyse.

Look at the example of a story ending from *Jessica's Other World* by David Waugh:

> *'What is it Mr Addison used to say all the time?' asked Jessica, but she answered her own question: 'It's make your mind up time!'*

Questions immediately arise. Who is Mr Addison? Who is Jessica? What does she have to make up her mind about?

Discuss story endings with children and ask them for their favourites. Ask what kind of endings they prefer. For example, do they like everything to be rounded off neatly so that we know what happens to everyone? Or do they prefer to be left wondering what happens next and wanting a sequel?

Show the children some examples and ask them to find more from their reading books and the class library. They then make notes, either individually or in pairs, on what they think might have happened in the story to lead up to the final line. Ensure that when the children have completed their notes, there are copies of the books available for them to read, to compare their notes with the real stories.

Taking it further

You might go on to give the whole class the same story ending as a starting point for their writing, having ensured that no one already knows the story. Alternatively, you could find a selection of endings from unfamiliar stories, but give these out according to children's interests. Ask them to make notes on what they think led up to the final sentence and to write some passages from their own version.

IDEA 45

Prompts for oral storytelling

'I want my class to think about story structure and to be able to tell stories orally.'

Being able to tell a story without reading it is an important skill, and one which we use in everyday life when relating events which happened to us or even when telling jokes. This activity helps to provide a structure and prompts for telling stories.

This activity could be linked to Idea 42 (six-word stories), which also shows how a longer story can be condensed into a few words.

Find some stories which you can tell confidently without reading them, such as *Jack and the Beanstalk*, *The Three Little Pigs* and *Cinderella*. Make some brief notes which you can display for the children, so they can see how you use these to guide your storytelling.

Begin by telling a story to the class as they look at your brief notes. Afterwards, ask them to use the notes to tell each other the story. Encourage them to discuss each other's versions and to suggest what might be added, changed or removed.

Next, ask the children to work in pairs to make brief notes about the sequence of events in a well-known story such as a fairytale. Then ask them to practise telling it, first to each other and then to other pairs of children.

Taking it further

As children become more proficient at telling stories using only brief notes to prompt them, you might plan a performance for other classes or have pairs of your pupils work with pairs of younger children to tell them stories. Talk with the children about the importance of using expression and varying their voices so that they engage the people who are listening to them.

Other-world stories

'My children love the Narnia stories and want to read more tales in which characters discover new worlds.'

In this activity there is a focus on stories in which characters are transported into another world. Children discuss and write part of a story in which this happens.

This is a common genre, with examples including C. S. Lewis's *The Chronicles of Narnia*, Philippa Pearce's *Tom's Midnight Garden*, Lewis Carroll's *Alice's Adventures in Wonderland* and even David Waugh's *Jessica's Other World*.

After introducing the theme of other-world stories, ask children to discuss and make notes on stories in which characters are transported between worlds. They can consider Alice travelling through the looking glass or Lucy going through the wardrobe. Once this is complete then the children, in preparation for writing a section of their own 'other world' story, can make notes on each of the following descriptions:

- The characters who will feature in their stories.
- The place in which the story begins.
- The move from one world to another.
- The reactions of the characters on reaching another world.
- What the new world looks like.

Encourage children to discuss their ideas with each other and to make suggestions of ways in which the story could be improved and developed.

Bring them together to share ideas and to draw out interesting and useful vocabulary. You may wish to introduce or remind them of words like 'secret', 'mysterious', 'peculiar', 'different', 'strange' and 'trepidation'.

Teaching tip

Discuss other-world stories with children and ask them for examples. Read some extracts from books which tell of characters' first transfers between worlds, how they achieved this and their initial reactions to the new worlds.

Taking it further

Work towards children making plans that will enable them to write a complete short story.

IDEA 47

Different points of view

'[Pupils] should have opportunities to compare characters, consider different accounts of the same event and discuss viewpoints (both of authors and of fictional characters), within a text and across more than one text.' (English National Curriculum)

In this activity children are encouraged to look at stories from different characters' perspectives.

Read at least one example of a familiar story told from a different person's point of view. There are lots of examples of often humorous versions of familiar stories in which the usual hero's status is changed. Roald Dahl's *Revolting Rhymes*, for example, provides alternative versions of traditional tales such as *Goldilocks and the Three Bears* and *Little Red Riding Hood*.

Ask children to discuss the changes made to the stories. Talk about the ways in which vocabulary and phrasing are used to portray characters in a different light.

Try hot-seating, with children taking on the roles of characters and answering questions, to show that different characters sometimes give different answers.

Ask children to retell a familiar story from a different perspective. Encourage them to focus on key events in the story and to write these so that traditionally 'good' characters become bad and vice versa. It will be helpful if you get children to pause every so often so that you can model some writing with the class and show the kinds of adjectives, adverbs and verbs which might be used to convey an image of a character. For example, unpleasant characters may sneer, grovel, moan or cackle, while more pleasant ones may smile, support, sympathise or chuckle.

Taking it further

Read some of the children's stories aloud and display them, discussing the use of language and the effect it has upon readers.

Sweets

'I want a lesson which children will enjoy and which will help me to establish my role with a new class.'

This is a highly structured activity which can be undertaken with any age group, where children have to write about the experience of eating a sweet. Not only does it lead to interesting descriptive writing, but it also allows the teacher to demonstrate classroom management skills in a positive way.

The ideal sweets for this activity are those with a contrasting centre, such as Smarties®. Start by showing the children the sweets and explaining that you will place one in front of each person, but no one must touch it.

Children then have a short time (perhaps two or three minutes) to write as quickly as possible what the sweet looks like. Encourage them to use similes ('as shiny as a button') and metaphors ('it is a tiny inviting pebble'), but tell them they don't have to write in full sentences at this stage.

Next, ask children to pick up their pens and then, when you give the order, they should pick the sweet up with the hand they don't use for writing and quickly write about what it feels like. Again, encourage adventurous language, interesting adjectives, similes and metaphors.

Then tell the children that they are now going to do the hardest part of the task. When you give the word, they must put their sweets in their mouths and suck but not crunch them. They should write about what it feels and tastes like to suck the sweet until you tell them to crunch it, and then immediately write about the crunching experience.

Finally, ask children to share their ideas and descriptions for each of the four stages.

Teaching tip

Before this lesson, you need to check that the school is happy for children to eat a sweet in class and that no children are allergic to them. If necessary, amend the lesson to use a healthier foodstuff, but be aware that there may be children who won't want to eat grapes, and so on.

Taking it further

Ask children to describe the 'sweet experience' in four lines so that anyone reading their work would immediately recognise the experience.

IDEA 49

Writing for younger children

'I want to give my class a real audience for their writing.'

This activity requires children not only to consider narrative structure, but also to think about the vocabulary and phrasing they use, since they will be writing for younger pupils.

Teaching tip

Find lots of examples of stories written for younger children. Create a presentation so that you can show the whole class samples of text and discuss them.

Taking it further

A development could be to create a book of short stories to include in class libraries.

Ask the children to read some stories and to discuss the features which make them appealing to younger readers. For example, the songlike language, use of repetition and dialogue between characters in *The Gruffalo* by Julia Donaldson.

Bring the class together and use the children's ideas to create a chart which shows some of the elements of successful stories. For example: a good storyline, interesting characters, a good story opening, an interesting setting, accessible vocabulary and style, colourful illustrations, and a happy ending.

Children can then work individually or in pairs to create their own stories that are aimed at younger readers. These might be based on their own original ideas or could be retellings of traditional tales. Encourage discussion and stop the class occasionally to enable children to share their stories and receive feedback.

Ask the children to read their finished stories to a younger class. The stories may be in continuous prose, but a variation could be to produce a PowerPoint presentation with imported pictures and limited text, so that children can tell the stories orally and then get the younger pupils to use the slides as prompts to tell the stories themselves.

A wish

'I wish I could think of a writing activity which would stimulate some of my reluctant writers.'

Children describe making a wish and having it granted.

Discuss examples of wishes and ask the children to consider what they would wish for if they were presented with the opportunity. The wishes could be for a permanent change to something, but you may find it best to focus on wishes for experiences that don't involve permanent change, such as meeting a famous person, playing in an important match or eating a wonderful meal.

Ask the children to research and make notes on some of the people and things that will appear in their wishes. For example, if they wished to meet a celebrity, they could find out about the person so they could describe the conversation and experience in detail.

Encourage them to write about their feelings as they experience their wishes. They could write a complete narrative which describes their initial response, the actual experience and how it made them feel afterwards.

Teaching tip

There are lots of examples of wishes being granted in traditional tales. E. Nesbit's classic *Five Children and It* gives excellent examples of how wishes can go horribly wrong. For more modern examples, look at *The Wishroom* by David Waugh. Ensure that children see and hear several examples of wishes before they begin to write.

Taking it further

You could develop the activity so that children talk to their families about wishes and write up their families' wishes to create a webpage or blog, or a class book of wishes.

IDEA 51

A moody opening

'You can tell this story is going to be scary!'

Children rewrite the opening lines of a book in a way that changes the mood of the story.

Teaching tip

Have a library session and allow the children to trawl through books to find their favourite opening lines. These can be recorded on large sheets and shared on a working wall for children to choose from.

The opening line of a book can grip a reader and set the scene and mood of the ensuing chapter. The infamous opening of *Charlotte's Web* by E. B. White does exactly this:

> *'Where's Papa going with that axe?' said Fern to her mother as they were setting the table for breakfast.*
> *'Out to the hoghouse,' replied Mrs Arable. 'Some pigs were born last night.'*

As the opening unfolds, Fern learns that Papa is going to 'do away' with one of the pigs. The mood is set. It's a horrifying prospect for Fern that her father is going to slaughter the piglet. But imagine if Mrs Arable's response was a different one. The mood at the start of the story could have been very different.

> *'Where's Papa going with that axe?' said Fern to her mother as they were setting the table for breakfast.*
> *'To chop some wood for the fire,' replied Mrs Arable. 'We can cuddle up in front of the hearth and play games when it's lit.'*

The mood here is very different and paints a warm fuzzy feeling of family life.

Give the children a range of opening lines and ask them to change the mood of the writing. This way, children can practise the skill in an engaging way before applying it in their own writing. Children could make a sad opening happy or a dangerous opening comedic, or maybe take one opening and create a number of different moods from it.

Before they all lived happily ever after

'Let's start at the very beginning, a very good place to start.' (Maria in *The Sound of Music*)

Children tell a story backwards, by starting at the end and working back to the beginning.

Ask children to think about fairytales. Do they usually end with something along the lines of, 'And they all lived happily ever after'? But what happened before this? Starting at the end of the story and working backwards allows children to practise using conjunctions such as 'before', 'previously' and 'earlier'.

Examine an example of a 'backwards' story with the children (such as the one below), and discuss the conjunctions, punctuation and structures used. Children can then create their own 'before' story.

> *And they all lived happily ever after.* ***Before*** *this, a relieved little old lady was being pulled safely from beneath the bed where she had been hiding in her frilly pyjamas.* ***Previously****, a woodcutter had used his huge axe and smashed down the front door to save the young cloak-wearing girl.* ***Moments earlier****, the wolf had leapt from the bed baring its big teeth to pounce on the girl.* ***Just before this happened****, the girl had been admiring the teeth, eyes and ears of the wolf, whom she had foolishly mistaken for her grandmother.* ***Beforehand****, she had wandered through the forest carrying a basket of treats for the old woman.* ***Once upon a time before all of this happened****, there was just a girl, who lived in a cottage in the forest with her mother, called Little Red Riding Hood.*

Teaching tip

Some children could be supported by having a simple narrative on strips that they can reorder on a small dry-wipe board. They can write the conjunctions between each strip once they have changed the order.

IDEA 53

Multiperspectivity

'You don't need your eyes to love, right? You just feel it inside you. That's how it is in heaven. It's just love, and no one forgets who they love.' (R. J. Palacio, *Wonder* – a story told through multiple perspectives)

Practise telling a story from multiple characters' viewpoints.

Multiperspectivity is a narratological tool which can be employed by authors in order to show the same story through the eyes of a number of characters. Although at first it may seem like a complicated writing structure, it is, in fact, a narrative for children to understand and use.

Generally, most children's books are told either in the first person character voice or in the third person by an omnipresent narrator. These stories are usually told from the point of view of the main protagonist throughout (although there are some notable exceptions to this).

There are a number of books told through multiple perspectives that are suitable for use in the primary classroom, including:

- *Voices in the Park* by Anthony Browne
- *The Day the Crayons Quit* by Drew Daywalt
- *Wonderstruck* by Brian Selznick
- *The Candymakers* by Wendy Mass
- *Wonder* by R. J. Palacio.

In *Wonder* the story is told over eight parts. Each part is told by a different narrator, switching between: August (Auggie), the main protagonist; Via, Auggie's older sister; Auggie's classmates, Summer and Jack; and Via's boyfriend, Justin. The novel explores Auggie's facial disfigurement through the reactions of these characters to it.

This technique can be developed by reading simple narratives and then adding a second,

Teaching tip

There are a number of short animations on www.literacyshed.com which only have two characters so children can tell the story from opposing viewpoints. These include:

- *Pigeon Impossible*
- *French Roast*
- *Ruckus*
- *Replay*
- *Road's End.*

third or even a fourth narrative voice. It is prudent to choose a story with which the children are familiar, such as a simple fairytale told in the third person.

> *Rapunzel let down her hair so that Prince Charming, who was waiting below, could climb up it.*

In this example we don't know how Rapunzel or Prince Charming feel about this. The children could give them a voice and rewrite this short section in the first person.

> Rapunzel: *I saw my hero waiting below. 'Lower your hair,' he called out to me, 'so I can climb up it.' 'Climb up my hair?' I thought, 'This guy is crazy!'*
>
> Prince Charming: *I arrived at the tower forthwith and saw the beauty with the golden hair sitting at the window high above the ground. I thought for a moment and then came up with a stupendous plan. Climb up her hair! 'Hey, hang your hair out of the window,' I shouted to her, but I don't think she heard me as she just looked down blankly.*

Once the children have practised retelling a narrative from differing viewpoints, these viewpoints can then be weaved into a third-person narrative. Imagine the scene when the prince arrives at the home of Cinderella with the glass slipper. The narrator can describe the scene and then the ugly sisters could give their point of view through an internal monologue, followed by the prince's thoughts on how ugly they are, before the reader can see Cinderella's inner turmoil at revealing her secret.

Stories with a hero and villain, such as *George and the Dragon*, give the opportunity for children to tell a story from diametric viewpoints (in this case, the anti-dragon narrative voiced by George and the defence of his actions by the dragon).

Bonus idea ★

The children could look at the Charlie and Lola books by Lauren Child and tell the story from opposite viewpoints. In *I Will Not Ever Never Eat a Tomato* the children could have Charlie explain how he helped Lola or have Lola explain how she tricked Charlie.

IDEA 54

Being or non-being: such is my dilemma

'Noon rings out. A wasp, making an ominous sound, a sound akin to a klaxon or a tocsin, flits about. Augustus, who has had a bad night, sits up blinking and purblind.' (Georges Perec, *A Void*)

Try to write a sentence without using one letter of the alphabet.

Do you notice anything unusual about the quote above? There is no letter 'e' used. In fact, there is no letter 'e' used at all in the whole book of 300 pages.

Restricting children's writing by banning specific letters stops them from scribbling the first word that pops into their head. If you think of the example above where the letter 'e' is banned, then words such as 'the', 'because', 'he' and 'she' become unavailable. The writer has to think of alternative words.

Ask children to rewrite a sentence while omitting a single letter. For example, try writing 'Harry Potter went to Hogwarts School' without using the letter 'o'.

Responses will be varied. Many children leave out 'Potter' and change 'Hogwarts School' to a descriptive phrase such as 'Harry attended a magical academy'. But who is this Harry? The original was specific. As children edit their sentences to be more specific, the structure changes: 'The famed juvenile wizard, Harry...' (expansion before the subject); 'Harry, the scarred wizard, attended...' (appositive added). By placing a restriction on a single letter, the original sentence can become much more developed: 'Harry, the scarred wizard, was trained in the magical arts at an acclaimed wizardry and witchcraft academy.'

Teaching tip

The title of this idea is one of the most famous phrases in the English language but with a restriction on the letter 't'. Can you identify it? (Answer: Shakespeare's *Hamlet*).

Bonus idea ★

You could give each group of children a different vowel that they have to miss out. One group has to miss out 'a', another 'e', and so on. They could then be given the challenge to write a Harry Potter character description and compare each other's to see how each group's differ or are similar.

Anthropomorphism

'Stories belong to the teller,' says the bard. 'At least half of them do. The other part belongs to the listeners. When a good story is told to a good listener, the pair of them own it together.' (Kieran Larwood, *The Legend of Podkin One-Ear*)

Some of the greatest stories for children include animals with human-like qualities. Allowing children to write stories with their own anthropomorphic characters is another way of creating stories and encouraging writing.

When thinking about characteristics of animal characters, it may be that they have similar traits to their natural counterparts. A mouse may be nervous, a rabbit timid and a fox sly. It is also fun to have characters who defy these usual traits. It may be that the hero mouse is brave and adventurous, while the lion is cowardly.

Children could also try bringing to life inanimate objects such as crayons and houses. It is an engaging activity to give these objects a voice. In Drew Daywalt's *The Day the Crayons Quit*, the coloured crayons write to complain at their perceived misuse by their owner. This can lead to various questions. Does the TV like sitting in the corner of the room for days on end? Is your house happy about everything that goes on inside it? Does your pencil like maths or does it prefer story-writing and why?

Other recent texts with anthropomorphic characters include:

- *The House with Chicken Legs* by Sophie Anderson
- *The Legend of Podkin One-Ear* by Kieran Larwood
- *Varjak Paw* by S. F. Said
- *The Umbrella Mouse* by Anna Fargher.

Teaching tip

Classic texts with anthropomorphic characters include:

- *The Wind in the Willows* by Kenneth Grahame
- *The Animals of Farthing Wood* by Colin Dann
- *Stuart Little* by E. B. White
- *Charlotte's Web* by E. B. White.

Bonus idea 

Use the app ChatterPix Kids to bring an inanimate object to life by adding animated eyes and a mouth which will repeat anything that is spoken into it. That way the children can actually become the voice of the object.

IDEA 56

Pick 'n' mix

'Life is like a box of chocolates. You never know what you're gonna get.' (Forrest Gump)

Imagine the results if we treated the writing process like a lucky dip into a chocolate box. In this activity, children choose characters and settings at random as a basis for their original narratives.

Choose a number of stock characters, settings and objects to be placed into a box or bag so that children can choose them at random. Children enjoy telling stories with odd matches, such as 'The pirate in the rainforest with an umbrella' or 'The wise old elf in a lighthouse with a treasure chest'. Mixing genres can work but it is more difficult for some children. For example, a robot from the year 3042 finding the gingerbread house in the forest may present itself as a challenge.

Ask the children to answer these simple questions. Why are they there? How did they get there? What are they going to do next? Ask them to share their answers with the rest of the class. Once a number of children have shared their answers then model how to create a short narrative from the answers.

It may be that your wise old elf is in the lighthouse watching for a pirate ship. The pirates have kidnapped one of the elves and the treasure chest contains the ransom money. Share your writing process with the children and allow them to have input into the narrative. During this shared writing activity, the teacher can add in any grammar points or writing techniques that have been covered previously, such as building tension, show: don't tell, or using similes and metaphor.

Teaching tip

Hand out magazines, catalogues and holiday brochures, and ask children to cut out their favourite characters and settings as well as finding them online. These can be then stored in bags ready for the children to select at random.

The writing collective

'I couldn't think of any great similes for my description, so I read the others and joined together two that I liked.'

Encourage children to collect ideas from their peers in order to improve their own writing.

Most adult writers will have a wealth of language to draw upon, often developed through a lifetime of reading. They may have even made notes while reading books as inspiration for their writing. It is safe to say that primary children will not have read as many books as their favourite authors and will have a lack of language experience to draw upon. The National Curriculum states that children should think aloud as they are collecting ideas – when they are thinking out loud then it may be useful for some children to be listening to and developing those ideas.

There are a number of ways for them to collect and share ideas with their peers. Here is an example using similes:

- Children create a simile to describe a particular setting on a whiteboard or sticky note.
- In pairs, children read their similes to each other, listening carefully.
- They then swap similes and take their new simile to someone else, to read out again.
- This process can continue until children have swapped and read out a number of different similes.

Reading this range of similes and rehearsing them orally should encourage children to use them in their own writing. As part of this activity you may wish to discuss which of the similes are more effective than others and why.

Teaching tip

If the similes are written on sticky notes they can then be collated on a working wall or window in the classroom so that children can revisit them throughout their independent writing time.

IDEA 58

Short sentences. They add something.

'This sentence has five words. Here are five more words. Five-word sentences are fine. But several together become monotonous. Listen to what is happening. The writing is getting boring. The sound of it drones. It's like a stuck record. The ear demands some variety.' (Gary Provost)

Children practise using short sentences for dramatic effect.

Two- or three-word sentences can be used to show panic, danger or tension or to show heightened emotion.

Read this section of a version of *Little Red Riding Hood*:

> *She heard the noise again; footsteps behind her in the darkness of the forest. She hurried and her feet made little impression on the soft, leaf-littered ground. There was rustling to her left so she ran as fast as her little legs would carry her.*

Then contrast it with this version below:

> *There it was again... footsteps. She hurried. Her feet made little impression on the soft, leaf-littered ground. There was rustling to her left. She ran.*

The short sentences force the reader to read at pace and to feel the tension and panic of Little Red Riding Hood.

Ask the children to take a scene from a book that is written in long descriptive sentences. Ask the children to rewrite the scene with shorter sentences for dramatic affect. Compare the two descriptions by reading both to their peers.

Teaching tip

It is important you demonstrate that a mix of sentences is needed, and that a piece of writing that only has very short sentences will not be as effective as one with a variety of sentences.

Taking it further

Can the children then write their own original description of being chased by a villainous character using short sentences?

IDEA 59

Non-linear adventure stories

'I used to stay up late every night making up stories under my duvet with a torch with these kind of books!'

Experiment with stories where readers choose what happens next.

Most narratives which children learn are linear in nature. However, in the 1970s and 1980s a range of stories became very popular both in book and computer-game format. These texts allowed the reader to take control of the story by giving them choices at the end of each section. They were very often adventure stories and went something like this:

> *They entered the cavern, one holding a torch and the other carrying the sword that he had rescued from the wizard earlier. They made their way along the dark passageway where something was glowing in the distance. They came to a tunnel that ran off at right angles, so dark they could only see a few feet into it. They carried on towards the glowing light. Suddenly, the light grew stronger and they could see in the fiery light a dragon breathing fire from its nostrils.*
>
> *What do they do next? Go and confront the dragon? Turn to page 37. Try the dark tunnel instead? Turn to page 42.*

You can support your children in writing these stories by giving them a writing scaffold in the form of a flow diagram which branches off as they move through the story. This diagram can be a simple framework by which readers choose between two choices once or twice in the narrative, or it may be more complex with multiple choices leading to a range of endings.

Teaching tip

Present the stories as PowerPoint presentations with hyperlinks in order to make them interactive. For example, 'Click here to fight the dragon' takes you to the dragon slide. 'Click here to run away' links to a different slide in the story.

IDEA 60

Fan fiction

'I wish I'd written *Harry Potter* because now I'd be a millionaire!'

Freeing children to write about familiar things can help those who struggle to conjure up new settings and characters.

Taking it further

You could explore fan fiction written by others with the children through websites such as www.wattpad.com and www.fanfiction.net.

Unshackle children from the bonds of originality and free them to write about things they are already familiar with in order for them to be more engaged in the writing process.

Fan fiction is a great opportunity for the novice writer because it arms them with fully formed characters and worlds. The familiarity means that the children can focus on vocabulary, sentence structures and plot, while setting and character arcs are broadly already in place.

You can scaffold this writing process by immersing the children in an imaginary world. One example could be the world of young offenders, ruthless guards and searing heat at Camp Green Lake: a world invented by Louis Sachar in the novel *Holes*.

When reading the novel or watching the film, children can discuss character traits and how the characters interact with each other. They can consider how these characters would act if they were placed in a new scenario or introduced to a new character.

If children decide to introduce a new character, there are a number of writing outcomes that can be achieved, including:

- A new character intervening in an existing episode.
- Dialogue between the new character and an existing one.
- A retelling of an exciting scene through the eyes of a new character.

Language

IDEA 61

Adverbs

'I want my class to use adverbs more effectively.'

This activity shows how adverbs can be used to enhance writing and make it clear to the reader how certain things are done. Although the aim is to encourage children to make greater use of adverbs, they should also realise that it's not necessary to use an adverb every time they use a verb.

Begin by reading a story to the children, but take out all the adverbs. Ask the children if they think they could make it more exciting by improving the descriptions. Draw from them the idea that adverbs can help the reader by showing how things are done.

To reinforce this idea, ask children to take turns to perform simple tasks and ask the rest of the class to provide adverbs to describe how the children performed them. For example, they could walk 'quietly', hop 'madly', smile 'widely', laugh 'hysterically', jump 'enthusiastically' or write 'quickly'.

Then ask children to work together to add adverbs where appropriate to a text; perhaps the story you first read out to them, or something you've prepared especially for this activity. They need not rewrite the whole text out themselves; they could simply insert a caret (a mark to show where something should be inserted) in the place where they would like to place an adverb and then write the word above the line. Ensure the text is double spaced to make this possible.

Emphasise that it's not necessary to use an adverb for every verb, and they should concentrate on those verbs which they think would benefit most from some additional description.

Teaching tip

Find some examples of the effective use of adverbs in a story which is currently being read to the children. Make a display of common verbs accompanied by examples of adverbs which could go with them, and sentences which contain the verbs and adverbs.

Taking it further

Some children could write their own introductory paragraphs for the story, using their own verbs as well as adverbs. Discuss ways in which sentences can be restructured so that adverbs appear at the beginning. Explore adverbial phrases as sentence openers. Some children may benefit from being given a list of possible adverbs, which they could choose from to insert into the story.

Name that road!

'Where the streets have no name.' (U2)

This activity provides an opportunity to develop vocabulary knowledge linked to particular themes. Children invent the street names for a new estate, linked to a particular theme such as trees, flowers or birds.

Use a digital map to show the children their locality. Talk about the different names that exist for streets and explain some of them (for example, avenues are usually tree-lined and crescents tend to be crescent-shaped like a new moon). Ask the children about the names of the streets they live on and discuss how these might have come about.

Ask the children to help you to think of some alternative names for their streets based on local features. Show them how to write the names, using capital letters for both the name and the type of street. For example, Oak Road, Cornwall Street or Hawthorn Terrace.

Then explain that you have a map of a new estate and you would like the children to make up names for its streets. Discuss the fact that many estates have street names which follow a theme and that all the streets might, for instance, be named after birds, trees or flowers. Children could use the various names for 'street', such as 'road', 'avenue', 'crescent' and 'lane'.

When they have made a list using capitals at the beginnings of words followed by lower case and have had their spellings checked, ask them to label the map.

Teaching tip

Provide lists of the names of flowers, birds or other things to help children carry out the task. You could also ask the children to make use of dictionaries, atlases and other reference sources to find names for the streets.

Taking it further

Some children could go on to look at maps of their locality or nearby towns and devise alternative names for some of the streets. Alternatively, they could think of new names for the streets in the board game Monopoly™.

IDEA 63

Varying adjectives

'Nice to see you... to see you, delightful!'

Children are presented with a passage of text in which rather mundane adjectives have been used. They are asked to think about ways in which the text could be enlivened by the use of more interesting adjectives that enable the reader to gain a clearer picture of the scene.

Teaching tip

Write a short passage in which the only adjective used is 'nice'. Alternatively, you might restrict the adjectives to words like 'good', 'nice', 'lovely' and 'fine'.

Taking it further

Some children could go on to write further text. Encourage them to be adventurous in their use of adjectives.

In preparation for this activity, you'll need to write a short passage of text that only uses common and repeated adjectives. Read this passage to the children and then ask them to tell you about it. Ask them to describe the scene and encourage them to use adjectives to do so.

Help the children to understand how to use adjectives by asking them to think of adjectives which describe different items in the classroom. Ask, 'Who can think of an adjective to describe...?'

Once the children have a clear idea of what an adjective is, ask them to look at the passage again with you and identify the adjectives as they read the text with you. Ask them if they can suggest alternative adjectives to those in the text so they can make it more interesting and can 'paint a better picture' with words.

Provide the children with copies of the text and ask them to substitute their own adjectives for those in the passage whenever they feel they could improve it. They may wish to add extra adjectives so that some nouns acquire an adjective and some are now described by two or more adjectives.

What's the question?

'To be or not to be, that is the question.' (Shakespeare, *Hamlet*)

Children are asked to create questions to go with answers that you or other children provide. The objective is both to develop their knowledge and their ability to formulate and write questions accurately.

Start by writing some 'answers' on the board and ask the children to think of questions which would lead to those answers. For example, the answer '12 square metres' might produce the question: 'What is the area of a rectangle which is 4 metres long and 3 metres wide?' And the answer 'Henry VIII' might produce the question: 'Which king had six wives?'

Then produce some 'answers' on pieces of card and give these out. Explain to the children that they need to create appropriate questions to match each answer. The questions need to begin with capital letters and end with question marks.

Tell the children that they can write whatever questions they wish as long as they produce the answers provided. Encourage them to check facts in texts and online where appropriate.

Teaching tip

Draw on topics you've recently covered across the curriculum when creating your answers so that you reinforce the children's learning.

Bonus idea ★

After the writing part of the lesson, you might organise a quiz using the questions and answers. This could even be a 'backwards quiz' in which contestants are given the answers and then have to make up a question.

Plurals

'Some of my children get into a muddle when using plurals. How can I help them?'

Regular plurals in English are formed by adding an 's' to the singular form. Most children have worked this out orally and apply the rule in speech even before they start school. However, there are many exceptions to the rule and it is these which present problems and often cause amusement. This activity is intended to introduce the terms 'singular' and 'plural', and to provide children with the opportunity to look at some common irregular plurals.

Teaching tip

Begin by using tangible items such as chairs, pencils, books and even children to ask children to give singulars and plurals. They will find this simple, especially if you stick to regular plurals.

Write the headings 'singular' and 'plural' on the board and ask the children to give examples of singulars, which you can write down on the board. Then ask them to give you examples of plurals and write these in a parallel column.

Ask the children to tell you what the rule is for turning singulars into plurals, and then ask them if there are any exceptions. You could start by asking what the plural of 'child' is.

Go on to look at sets of plurals which conform to rules. For example:

- Brushes, bushes, watches, churches.
- Tomatoes, potatoes, echoes, heroes.
- Babies, ladies, lilies, stories.
- Monkeys, donkeys, keys.
- Lives, wives, loaves, leaves.

Ask the children to try to work out what the rules are for the sets of plurals and encourage them to look closely at the words to find out what distinguishes one type of word from another. For example, get them to look at the words which end with 'h' (the first set in the list above) and ask them how the plural is formed. Then write a rule such as 'words which end with "h" add "es" when they are made into plurals'.

To help the children to work out the plurals of words ending with 'y' (the third and fourth sets in the list opposite), you could teach them that the word 'key' is the key to remembering. They should all know that the plural of 'key' is 'keys' not 'kies', and if they remember that then they should be able to work out that words which have a vowel before the 'y' add an 's' in the plural (such as 'donkeys'), but words with a consonant drop the 'y' and add 'ies' (such as 'babies').

Can the children expand each list by adding more words which follow the same plural rule? They could work with a partner to write an additional word per pair.

Taking it further

Some words are the same in the plural and the singular. These include the names of most fish (or is it fishes?) and some other animals such as sheep. Some children could research these plurals and might make a collection using dictionaries and later asking adults at home.

IDEA 66

Subordinate clauses and phrases

'I want my children to use complex sentences to make their writing more varied and interesting.'

Introduce children to subordinate clauses and phrases with the following steps.

Steph was a brilliant footballer. She was captain of England.

These two sentences could be combined into one by using a subordinate clause, to make the writing less stilted.

Steph, who captained England, was a brilliant footballer.

Show the children examples of sentences which include subordinates, and ask them to look at them closely and read them aloud. Encourage them to look at the punctuation and ask them what the main messages in the sentences are. Ask them which part of the sentences are less important and explain to them that these are subordinates.

Show some more sentences and ask them to identify the subordinates. Then show them some sentences which don't have subordinates, and ask them to think of phrases or clauses which they could add. Emphasise the need to use commas to separate the main clause from the subordinate.

Write a series of pairs of related sentences on the board and ask children to try to combine the sentences in each example.

Teaching tip

It's important to explain:

- 'Subordinate' means less important or lower down the order.
- A clause contains a verb.
- A phrase doesn't contain a verb.
- The word that connects the clause to the main sentence is a relative pronoun (for example, 'who', 'which', 'whose') or a subordinating conjunction (for example, 'but', 'while').

Bonus idea ★

Stop the class occasionally to draw attention to the different ways in which children have approached the task. Write some of their sentences on the board and discuss them.

Verbs

'I'd like my class to vary the verbs they use in their writing.'

Children pick out the verbs in a text and then attempt to replace them with alternatives.

Show the children some sentences on the board and ask if anyone can tell you what was being done in each. You could ask children to do things and then write what they've done on the board and invite them to identify the verbs. For example, 'Jayden scratched his head' or 'Faizal whispered something to Emily'.

Discuss the verbs with the children and ask them to try to replace them with alternatives. The children involved could then act out the revised actions. For example, 'Jayden nodded his head' and 'Faizal shouted something to Emily'.

You may feel that it's worth discussing the tenses of the verbs with the children and asking them to provide replacements which are in the same tenses as the original verbs.

Provide sample sentences and ask children to replace the verbs. You could put these on a worksheet and let children write the new verbs above the originals.

Stop the class occasionally to discuss which verbs they've used. Pay special attention to any inventive and new vocabulary, and make a point of showing the children how to spell such words.

Next, ask children to work in pairs to write sentences for each other to change. For children who find the activity difficult, you could provide a selection of alternative verbs to choose from.

Teaching tip

Despite being the most common verb and the starting point for sentences when we learn a foreign language, the verb 'to be' is often the one children find hardest to identify. When trying to find a replacement for a part of the verb 'to be', children may have to change the tense rather than the verb, since to do otherwise would often render a sentence nonsensical.

Taking it further

You could also ask children to take a familiar piece of text and change some or all of the verbs and then read it to the class.

IDEA 68

Ambiguity

'Harry was going to pass the ball, but decided to shoot himself instead.'

Children are asked to look at sentences which, though generally grammatically correct, lead to confusion because of their structure. This provides an opportunity for children to develop an understanding of the ways in which clauses can be manipulated to achieve different effects.

Show the children some examples of confusing sentences or make up some of your own. Ask them to read the sentences and tell you what the writer is *trying* to convey, and what he or she has *actually* told the reader. Ask children to suggest other ways of phrasing the sentences, by moving clauses, changing the wording, or both. For example:

> *Chelsea travelled from York to Doncaster in her best suit.*
> *Wearing her best suit, Chelsea travelled from York to Doncaster.*
> *Chelsea wore her best suit when she travelled from York to Doncaster.*

Work on sentences until you feel that children can see where they might be confusing and are confident about attempting to change them.

Next, explain that you want the children to look at some sentences and decide what the author really meant to say and then rewrite them. The following may be useful:

- Mr Archer spent two hours shooting at his farm.
- Saffi hid from her sister in her pyjamas.
- Mrs Brown sailed to the Isle of Man in a blue dress.
- Elis taught his dog to do tricks better than his father.

Taking it further

Children who complete the work successfully could try making up their own confusing sentences for others to reorganise.

- Hayley had a third child called Edward.
- The boxer was a tall man with a broken nose called Henry.
- Helping himself to a cake, Logan walked to the door and popped it in his mouth.
- Kai opened the door in his pyjamas.

Children could change the order of the words or change the words themselves. Encourage them to make several attempts to change the sentences if they feel this is necessary. The emphasis should be on their ability to manipulate word order rather than attractive presentation at this stage.

Stop the class occasionally so that children can compare notes on their approaches to changing the sentences and so that you can offer help and guidance.

Bonus idea ★

As part of an art lesson, children could go on to draw cartoons which depict the ridiculous scenarios suggested by some of the confusing sentences.

IDEA 69

Cooperative writing using pictures

'I want an activity which encourages children to produce careful, imaginative descriptive writing.'

This activity is based on a collection of stimulating pictures, which children describe and then use to make a short piece of writing.

You'll need to prepare for this activity by collecting together some pictures, such as children playing on a beach, from magazines and colour supplements. Simply cut out a selection of pictures (adverts are particularly good and you can leave out references to products if you like) and then attach them to pieces of A3 paper.

Start by putting a large picture in the centre of the board. Explain that you would like the children to help you to produce a description of the picture, so that if it were displayed along with several others, anyone reading the description would be able to identify which picture it's referring to.

Look at the picture with the children and ask them to suggest short phrases to describe various features. For example, for a beach scene: 'clear, blue sky', 'white, sandy beach', 'crashing, white waves', and 'bright, orange sun'. Write the children's suggestions in the space around the picture and continue to add to these as they have more ideas.

Ask the children to discuss how they might turn some of the phrases into sentences to produce a more refined piece of writing, perhaps combining phrases or adding further adjectives and adverbs. With the children's help, compose a short piece of descriptive writing to describe

Taking it further

Mount two large pictures on the board and explain to the children that you've written a short description of one of them. Ask them to listen carefully as you read your description and to wait until you've finished before deciding which of the two pictures you are describing, supporting their judgement by referring to what you wrote. Display the description so they can refer to it.

the picture. This could be prose, perhaps with a word limit of 50 words, or a poem with or without rhyme.

Next, provide each pair of children with a picture mounted on A3 paper and ask them to work together to make notes on the paper around the picture with descriptive phrases. These could include feelings generated by the picture, as well as descriptions of what can be seen.

After a few minutes, ask each pair to pass their picture and notes on to another pair, but not to discuss what they've written or to draw attention to errors. Ask the new pairs to look at what has already been written and then to add their own ideas.

Pass the pictures and notes on once more after a few minutes for further additions from another pair of children. Then ask the children to return the pictures to their original owners, and allow some discussion between all six of the writers involved.

Explain that the original writers can now draw upon everyone's ideas to help them to produce a short descriptive piece of writing. Tell them that you'll be displaying all of the pictures and all of the pieces of writing, but not next to each other. The writers need to make their descriptions good enough for readers to be able to match them to the appropriate pictures.

Bonus idea ★

This activity can be done as part of work in a range of subjects. For example, for history a selection of pictures related to a period about to be studied can serve to alert children to prior knowledge, as well as to raise questions about the period. The pictures used could be prints of famous paintings or paintings by a particular artist (these can be found cheaply in books in discount bookshops, or on the internet), and the activity might be linked to art appreciation.

IDEA 70

Comparative and superlative adjectives

'Some ideas are good; others are better. I want the best for my class!'

Adjectives can be used not only to describe nouns, but also to show degrees of intensity. This activity focuses on the varied use of adjectives for different effects for descriptive purposes.

Show the class a varied selection of images of animals, such as a giraffe, a dolphin, or an ant. Ask one child to come to the front to choose an animal and, with the help of the whole class, ascribe adjectives to describe the animal's measurable features (for example, 'the giraffe is tall').

Now ask a second child to come out to select an animal and ask the children to use the same adjectives to compare the two. Almost inevitably someone will suggest that one animal is the 'tallest' or the 'lightest'. Explain that one is 'taller' or 'lighter' and that the suffix we use when comparing two animals is '-er'.

Invite a third child to the front and ask children to use the adjectives to compare the three animals, explaining that we use '-est' when more than two people or things are being compared. You may wish to look at other adjectives such as 'happy' and 'angry', and look at the way in which they follow the rule. Children may suggest other adjectives which don't follow the same rule, such as 'good' and 'cheerful'. Make a note of these on the board and later add them to a display of comparative adjectives.

Explain that words ending in '-ful' have to be prefaced by 'more' when comparing two things and 'most' when comparing more than two. 'Good' changes to 'better' and 'best'.

Teaching tip

On cards or on the board, write a list of adjectives which relate to measurement. These could include: 'tall', 'heavy', 'light', 'short', 'small', 'big', 'old', 'young', 'long', 'wide' and 'fast'. Make some cards with the suffixes '-er' and '-est' written on them. Can the children then change the adjectives by using the appropriate suffix?

Taking it further

Ask the children to create their own sentences which include comparative adjectives. Stop the class occasionally to discuss answers and to reinforce the concept of comparative adjectives.

Bonus idea ★

Link this activity to work on measurement in mathematics.

Dialogue

IDEA 71

Fronted adverbials

'I'd like an activity which allows children to use adverbials in different ways, including beginning sentences with them.'

This activity can be done orally as well as in writing. It focuses on the use of a fronted adverbial and can include discussion about phrasing and punctuation.

Begin by saying a sentence to the children that starts with the word 'fortunately', such as, 'Fortunately, the rain has stopped.' Follow it with a sentence that begins with the word 'unfortunately', such as, 'Unfortunately, it is due to start again in about half an hour.'

Then try another sentence with 'fortunately' at the start, such as, 'Fortunately, I brought an umbrella to school today.' Ask the children to suggest a sentence beginning with 'unfortunately' that follows on well. For example, 'Unfortunately, my umbrella has a hole in it.'

When the children are confident about doing this, write some of their sentences on the board and talk about the spellings of 'fortunately' and 'unfortunately', and the importance of putting a comma after the fronted adverbial.

Now give them each a sheet of paper and ask them to write their own 'fortunately' sentence at the top. Then get them to pass these on so that another child writes an 'unfortunately' sentence underneath, before passing it back or on to another child. Keep the sequence going until everyone has a series of sentences that can be read aloud.

Talk about the vocabulary used and address any spelling or punctuation issues, before asking children to move on to other opposite adverbs.

Teaching tip

Make a collection of adverb opposites so you can develop and vary the activity. For example, 'sadly' and 'happily', 'nervously' and 'confidently', 'quickly' and 'slowly'.

Taking it further

You may go on to ask some children to use adverbial phrases at the beginnings of their sentences in their own writing, encouraging them to be more adventurous in their vocabulary and phrasing.

Letters from the teacher

'Getting to know you, getting to know all about you...' (Anna, *The King and I*)

This activity is great for getting to know a new class. You might use it when you meet a class in the summer term that you'll inherit in September, or to get to know children whom you will be teaching on a school placement.

Write a letter in which you tell children some things about yourself and ask questions about them. For example, you might tell them about your hobbies and favourite TV programmes, music and sports. After each thing you reveal about yourself, pose a question. For example, 'My favourite football team is Doncaster Rovers. Do you like football? If you do, what is your favourite team?'

When you've finished your letter, personalise it by putting 'Dear (child's name)' at the start so that every child's letter has his or her name on it. You might put the letters in envelopes or simply hand them out, being sure to learn children's names as you do so.

Ask children to read their letters, providing support for those who may find this difficult. Then ask them to write a reply after talking with them about how to set out a letter and reminding them about the need for question marks, and so on.

Once the children have 'sent' you their letters, read them carefully and make a few notes to remind yourself about the children's interests. This will provide you with lots to talk about when you meet them again and will help you to establish a good relationship with them. It'll also give you an insight into their writing abilities and alert you to things you need to do to support them once they are your own class.

Teaching tip

Create a bank of vocabulary which children might need for their letters and make it readily available for them to refer to, so they don't spend a lot of time asking you for spellings when they could be writing.

IDEA 73

Texting on paper

'A little less conversation, a little more action.' (Elvis Presley)

As they reach upper primary age, many children own mobile phones and are used to texting. However, schools rarely allow children to bring their phones into the classroom and the time-honoured practice of secretly passing notes continues. In this activity, note-passing is encouraged and children learn the etiquette and possible style of such communication.

Begin by writing a short message on the board and asking children how they would reply to it. For example, 'How are you feeling today?' or 'What's up?'. Talk about brevity and also about keeping in mind the 'audience' for such a message, and so using an appropriate, reader-friendly style.

Give children partners to correspond with and ask one of each pair to write a message to the other. This can then be read and responded to. Make it clear that the messages are not private and that you may be reading them.

Make it clear that this kind of communication should be concise and that longer messages would require a different style. The messages are not texts and so emojis and text-speak spellings aren't appropriate. However, you may decide to allow abbreviations and might make this a topic for discussion.

Talk with children about what they felt were the qualities of good messages and what they thought they could improve.

Teaching tip

There are lots of websites which give tips on texting etiquette and some of these may be worth discussing.

Taking it further

Write a mysterious note which suggests that someone may be about to do something wrong. Use this as a stimulus for writing. Children could speculate about what might happen and their stories could focus on catching the wrongdoers.

Imaginary dialogue

'I want to develop my class's use of dialogue through a creative activity.'

This activity is designed to get children to think carefully about well-known characters and the stories in which they appear. They then consider what conversations between characters from different stories might sound like.

Invite two children to act as the principal characters from two different stories, and ask them to hold a conversation with each other. To prepare for this, you might choose the children before the lesson and explain what they will be doing and ask them to think about what they might say to each other. The conversation could include references to their situations in their stories, so that, for example, Hansel might grumble about his awful stepmother, while Cinderella moans about her dreadful stepsisters.

Once children understand the activity, ask them to work in pairs or small groups to converse orally before going on to write dialogue or a script of the conversation. These can then be performed for the rest of the class, and teaching points can be made about writing direct speech and scripts.

Emphasise accurate punctuation of dialogue and model this for the class, using examples provided by the children.

Teaching tip

Provide several examples of well-known tales, such as *Goldilocks and the Three Bears, Little Red Riding Hood, Hansel and Gretel* and *Cinderella*. Discuss the stories and others which children are familiar with.

Bonus idea ★

Children could go on to write dialogue from imaginary interviews they hold with famous people, including historical characters or celebrities.

IDEA 75

Letter to the headteacher

'I want to focus on formal letter-writing through an activity in which children have a real recipient for their writing.'

Children compose letters about issues which are important to them. These might include the provision of play equipment, the school uniform, improving the school environment or playtime arrangements.

Teaching tip

Before starting this activity, discuss it with the headteacher and senior management team to ensure they are willing to respond to children's letters. They will be more likely to help if all the children write about the same theme, so they can write one letter in reply which incorporates responses to a range of issues raised.

Begin by holding a discussion about school-related issues that the children feel strongly about. Ask them to talk in pairs or small groups about their feelings and ideas about how things might be improved. Invite them to share their ideas with the class. Make notes on the board with key vocabulary available so they can refer to it when writing.

Ask the children to each write a letter to the headteacher, explaining what they think the school needs to change, and why. Explain that it's important to phrase their letters politely and to support views with evidence. Encourage the children to justify their suggestions, perhaps even including evidence from questionnaires given to classmates. Emphasise that it's important to present their letters in the correct format, neatly and accurately.

Before sending the letters to the headteacher or senior managers, explain that there may be good reasons why the children's suggestions might be impracticable and that they shouldn't necessarily expect changes to be made as a result of their letters. When replies are received, discuss these with the class and ask children to respond politely.

Bonus idea ★

A variation can be to write to school council representatives asking them to present the children's views at their meetings.

Making excuses

'The dog ate my homework, Miss.'

In this light-hearted activity, children explore imaginative excuses for failing to do things.

Begin by sharing some poetry or prose that has a theme of making excuses.

Three great examples are: 'Conversation Piece' by Gareth Owen (in the anthology *Poems to Perform*); 'All My Great Excuses' by Kenn Nesbitt (in the anthology *Revenge of the Lunch Ladies*); and 'Excuses' by Allan Ahlberg (in the anthology *Please Mrs Butler*).

After reading examples of excuses, ask the children to discuss in small groups some excuses they've made themselves or have heard others make and then share these with the class.

Next, ask them to think of some more fanciful excuses along the lines of those found in the poems mentioned above.

Make notes on the board to provide a word bank to support the children when working independently or in pairs. Ask children to write as many interesting excuses as they like and tell them that they can go on to 'perform' their excuses, perhaps having one child as the teacher while others take turns to offer excuses for failing to do things like homework, bringing PE kit to school or being late.

Taking it further

The performances might be practised and then presented to other classes and teachers. You could also create a class book of imaginative excuses.

IDEA 77

Script into direct speech

'I want an activity that focuses on accurate punctuation of direct speech.'

Children use a play script as a starting point for writing direct speech. They learn how to punctuate direct speech, and how to vary the verbs and adverbs used to indicate how words are spoken.

Teaching tip

You can find lots of free scripts online that are downloadable. Use an example to show how scripts are set out and to help you model converting script into direct speech.

Begin by showing an example of a play script to the children, such as the one below, and getting them to play different parts as you read it aloud.

Narrator: Goldilocks arrived at the prison and was met by two prison warders.

Warder A: So what did you do?

Goldilocks: I've been found guilty of breaking and entering.

Warder B: Is that all?

Goldilocks: And theft of, of –

Warder A: What?

Goldilocks: Three bowls of porridge.

Warder B: Three bowls? That seems a bit excessive.

Goldilocks: Well, you see, the first bowl was too hot.

Warder A: Yes?

Goldilocks: And the second bowl was too cold...

Warder B: Yes?

Goldilocks: But the third bowl was just right.

Warder A: Oh, I see.

Warder B: It still doesn't seem very evil.

Goldilocks: Well, there was also a little matter of wilful destruction of three chairs.

After reading the script, ask children to help you to write the first few lines as direct speech.

Emphasise the importance of beginning each person's speech on a new line, of using speech marks (inverted commas) around the words that are spoken, and of including punctuation before the closing speech marks.

Discuss how the lines in the script might have been spoken and invite the children to suggest appropriate verbs and adverbs. For example, for the script above they might suggest:

'So what did you do?' asked the first warder angrily.

'I've been found guilty of breaking and entering,' muttered Goldilocks nervously.

'Is that all?' said the second warder incredulously.

Taking it further

Look at lots of examples of dialogue in children's books and ask children to discuss how it's set out. They will find that it's not always necessary to state who is speaking, and that adverbs aren't always used to accompany verbs which describe how people are speaking.

IDEA 78

Direct speech into script

'The play's the thing...' (Shakespeare, *Hamlet*)

This activity can be done as part of a sequence of lessons including the previous idea ('Script into direct speech'). It involves looking at examples of dialogue and reading aloud, as well as converting dialogue into play scripts.

Teaching tip

The key learning outcome is for children to be able to identify the spoken word in dialogue and convert it into a play script, so you may wish to provide examples on computers so they can copy and paste dialogue rather than spending a lot of time writing everything out.

Taking it further

Children can go on to work independently, or in pairs or small groups, to convert examples of dialogue into scripts. You might then ask them to perform their scripts for the class.

Begin by involving children in shared reading by presenting a dialogue to the class and assigning roles to individual pupils. The whole class can read all of the text that is not within inverted commas, with the speech being read by those with roles. At first, you may find that some children make mistakes, so encourage them to look carefully for the inverted commas so they only read what they're supposed to read. You might try using the opening to David Waugh's story *Girls Can't Play Football!*, which starts with the lines:

> *'It's not a proper game if she plays!' Adam Stevens stood with his foot on the ball and his hands on his hips.*
>
> *'Go on, let her,' said Ryan Jones.*
>
> *Lauren Morris looked longingly towards the football pitch, where about twenty boys had stopped their game when she had asked to play.*

Once children are confident about identifying speech, model writing some text as a play script. Show how some parts, such as the line beginning 'Lauren Morris looked longingly...' might become stage directions or even be spoken by a narrator.

A written argument

'I want my class to develop their ability to write persuasively.'

In this activity there's a focus on persuasive language as children write about issues which interest them. This can lead from written arguments to full-scale debates.

Begin by writing a controversial statement on the board and asking the children to discuss it and then respond in writing. The statement could be something like:

> *Boys should not be allowed to play in the netball team.*
>
> *School should start at 8.00 am.*
>
> *School uniform should be bright yellow.*

Get children to read their responses aloud and write some of these on the board. Discuss vocabulary and phrasing that can be used to persuade people to agree with a point of view. You might create a chart for display which includes phrases such as: 'for this reason', 'it seems clear that', 'for instance', 'in addition', 'furthermore,' 'moreover' and 'undoubtedly'.

Encourage children to consider different points of view, perhaps asking them to defend an opinion which they don't actually hold. Ask them to work with partners to write statements and responses on issues. For example, each child in the pair could write a statement and then swap these with each other to write a response. Emphasise the importance of being persuasive, but also polite and reasonable.

At the end of the lesson, ask pairs of children to come to a conclusion on their opinions.

Taking it further

Hold a debate on some of the issues discussed. Ask some children to prepare speeches and others to prepare questions to ask the speakers.

IDEA 80

Using alternative verbs in dialogue

'My class tend to use "said" all the time when writing dialogue.'

This activity links to the previous two ideas and encourages children to think about alternatives to common verbs such as 'said'. It could also be linked to Idea 67 on varying verbs in writing.

Begin by reading a short passage of dialogue to the children. Explain that there are several different words which can be used instead of 'said' and read the passage again, asking children to spot these.

Now ask children to look at story books which include dialogue to see how many variations they can find for the word 'said'. Give them sheets with 'said' in the middle and ask them to write as many alternatives as possible around the word.

Next, ask children to look at other verbs to see how many alternatives they can find, such as 'whispered', 'gasped' and 'shouted'. They can do this through discussion first, but later they could use a dictionary or thesaurus.

Teaching tip

Make collections of interesting verbs from stories, poems and newspapers.

Taking it further

In subsequent lessons, ask children to draw upon their findings to vary their vocabulary in their writing.

Settings

Superhero Base

'Holy Superhero Base, Batman!'

This activity helps children to describe a setting through the objects that are in it rather than the surroundings themselves in four steps. It can be linked to Idea 25, where the children have already created a superhero and now describe a base, or it could be used as a solo activity.

Teaching tip

There are a few more seconds left in the animation which shows the pigeon being squashed by rocket debris. This part can be optional depending on the age of the class.

Show the children the animation 'Pigeon Impossible' from YouTube or the Fun Shed on the Literacy Shed website. Pause it once we meet the main character Walter Beckett as he sits on the bench to eat his breakfast. Ask the children what they think his job is. You may get answers like a spy, a secret agent or a superhero. Tell the children that he is a superhero but in disguise. Bearing this in mind, ask the children what might be inside the suitcase. Explain that you think it might be his superhero costume as he is currently wearing a suit and doesn't look much like a superhero. Then ask them to write and draw the clothes that they think might be in the case. They could include, for instance, a mask, gloves, boots, cape or pants outside of his trousers like Superman.

Play the animation again and pause it this time after the lasers, grenade launcher and rocket boosters have been seen. Tell the children that superheroes have lots of gadgets like these and more. Ask them to describe a superhero's gadgets, such as rocket boots, jet pack, binoculars or suction cup gloves.

Resume the animation and this time pause it when Walter zooms into the sky holding the suitcase. Explain that superheroes normally have better vehicles than suitcases and ask them for any examples they can think of such as the Batmobile, or the Milano jet from

Guardians of the Galaxy. Ask the children to draw a superhero vehicle, such as a submarine, motorbike, jet ski, helicopter or speed boat. Then the children can label this with the key features such as rocket launchers, lightning cannon or underwater mode.

Play the animation once more but stop it this time as Walter walks calmly away from the flaming cars and police sirens. Ask the children where they think he is going. Explain that he is returning to his superhero base and ask where they think this might be. Is it a cave like Batman's, or a mansion like the one in the X-Men comics? Ask the children to describe a superhero base location such as behind a waterfall, inside a volcano or in an underwater cave.

Taking it further

The children can then write a four-part description of a superhero setting including where it is, the vehicle that is parked there, what gadgets are there and what clothing can be seen.

IDEA 82

A flamboyance of flamingos

'A flock of flirting flamingos is pure, passionate, pink pandemonium – a frenetic flamingle-mangle – a discordant discothèque of delicious dancing, flamboyant feathers, and flamingo lingo.' (Charley Harper)

Ask children to create their own collective nouns for animals or people.

A collective noun is the word used to represent a group of people, animals or things. The more esoteric ones are often debased to a source of amusement and general-knowledge quiz questions. But there are some common collective nouns used in everyday language, such as:

- crowd
- committee
- band of musicians
- panel of interviewers
- pack of cards
- fleet of ships.

Collective nouns for animals are often less well known and are rarely used in spoken language or writing. Common examples of animal collective nouns are 'pack', 'flock', 'swarm' and 'herd'. These can be used for various creatures.

The words used for specific groups of animals are called 'terms of venery'. Many of these come from various 15th-century sources including the *Book of St Albans* written around 1486. These more spectacular examples include the following:

- flamboyance of flamingos
- dazzle of zebras
- tower of giraffes
- skulk of foxes
- circus of puffins
- troop of monkeys
- lounge of lizards.

Taking it further

Try using collective nouns as similes, as in the examples below.

- The gang prowled the estate like an ambush of tigers.
- The snowy mountains nestled together on the horizon like an aurora of giant polar bears.
- Models took to the catwalk like a flamboyance of flamingos.
- Schoolchildren alighted the coach like a troop of monkeys whooping and howling.

Ask children to create their own collective nouns by giving them a list of animals and a list of nouns. For example, you could give them animals such as snakes, tigers or eagles and give them nouns such as mountain, slime or crowd.

Not only are the terms of venery opposite a list of amusing language oddities, but they can also be used in narrative writing. Many of the phrases are evocative and can be used when writing setting descriptions to help convey a specific mood. For example, when creating a peaceful mood, perhaps to describe a quiet country walk, the following collective noun could be used:

> *As I crossed the dew-kissed meadow, the sun rose above the distant hills and a wisp of snipe took flight from the long reeds.*

The ephemeral word 'wisp' used here adds to the peaceful mood, whereas an example such as 'a pandemonium of parrots' or 'a band of plovers' would shatter the peace.

As well as creating peace, collective nouns could help writers to include some atmospheric language in their narratives. For example:

> *A murder of crows nestled on the black, skeletal branches above, almost invisible now the darkness had descended.*

The word 'murder' will have negative connotations for the reader, as would the word 'skulk' in the following example:

> *A skulk of foxes prowled through the town, illuminated only by the weak moonlight.*

Ask the children to choose a collective noun from the list opposite, or from an additional list that you provide, then write an atmospheric sentence using it.

Bonus idea ★

We asked on social media for examples of a collective noun for teachers and amongst our favourites were:

- an exhaustion of teachers
- a patience of teachers
- a reward of teachers
- an exaltation of teachers.

Can children come up with any more ideas?

IDEA 83

Painting settings with colour

'It is spring, moonless night in the small town, starless and bible-black, the cobblestreets silent and the hunched courters'-and-rabbits' wood limping invisible down to the sloeblack, slow, black, crowblack, fishingboat-bobbing sea.' (Dylan Thomas, *Under Milk Wood*)

In the opening quote above, Thomas develops the descriptive setting of the town using a single colour: black. The colour evokes an image of a deep darkness and a melancholy, mournful town. This activity will enable children to emulate this technique using a range of colours.

Taking it further

Find some landscape images where a single colour dominates. The children can add descriptive phrases to these before using the phrases in their setting descriptions.

Firstly, show a list of colours and discuss what colours mean to the children. What moods and emotions do they associate with each colour? For example, they might associate words such as 'dull', 'boring' and 'dreary' with the colour grey. Next, share some examples with the children of how these colours can make a reader imagine what certain places are like. For example, lush, green valleys might make us think of tropical rainforests.

Then ask the children to fill in the following scaffold grid with their own ideas. They should start by adding a colour and then move on to the setting, and so on.

My colour choice White (red a bit). **Setting idea** Log cabin in snowy woods. Red blood on ground to show something bad has happened.	**Synonyms or adjectives to describe the colour** • Pale • Icy • Colourless • Milky	**Nouns to describe the colour** • Sky • Clouds • Snowflakes • Frozen rivers

The children could use this grid to write a descriptive setting that focuses on using their chosen colour to help bring the scene to life.

Jumping in

'Jump!' (Van Halen)

By describing a setting in detail, children are able to set the scene and draw their reader into their story. You can help children to describe a setting they've never experienced or seen themselves by using images.

Choose an image for a scene you'd like the children to describe and share copies of this with the children. Encourage the children to imagine 'jumping into' the image by placing the image on the floor in front of them and stepping onto it.

Once the children have had some time to study and discuss the image, you can lead the children through the image by asking questions such as:

- Where are you?
- What can you see?
- Are the things you can see old-fashioned or modern?
- Are there any smells?
- What time of day is it? How does the light help you to decide this?
- What is the weather like? Is it hot or cold?
- What is the mood of this place? What makes you think this?
- Who else might be there? (They might not actually be in the image.) What are they doing?

You may want all children to have the same image so they can share their thoughts, or you could choose lots of images on the same theme (a beach scene, a mountainous landscape or a spooky forest). Children can then share their responses and create their own setting from the range of images, rather than directly describing the image they're looking at.

Teaching tip

Once children are familiar with this activity, allow them to create their own questions about the images, which they can then ask each other in small groups.

IDEA 85

All the world's a stage

'All the world's a stage...' (Shakespeare, *As You Like It*)

Creating extended metaphors for setting descriptions is the next logical step for young writers after they've had practice using isolated metaphors.

Teaching tip

In order for children to be able to develop and extend their use of metaphor, they'll need to have a working knowledge of metaphor. They'll need to know what makes an effective metaphor and the effect they can have on the reader, such as the difference between 'the moon is a football in the sky' and 'the moon is a wolf's eye watching the forest for prey'.

Firstly, pick a setting for the children to describe. Then ask them to think of things that it could be described as. For example: 'The forest is... a city.'

Brainstorm the objects and things you would find in each metaphor. So, a city may have skyscrapers, cars and motorways. Then link these things that appear in your metaphor to things that appear in your original setting. For example, you could link the metaphor of 'a city' to 'the forest':

- Trees are skyscrapers.
- Ants are people going to work.
- The river is a highway.

Once the children have created a bank of metaphors for their setting, it's time to turn this into a paragraph of descriptive writing.

You could remind children that it's not always necessary to say what's being described. In the example below, the words 'trees' and 'ants' aren't needed for the metaphors to be successful.

> *The rainforest is a city. Bark-covered skyscrapers tower up to the sky above, while tiny commuters crawl up and down their trunks with leaves loaded on their backs.*

Pathetic fallacy

'About midnight, while we still sat up, the storm came rattling over the Heights in full fury. There was a violent wind, as well as thunder...' (Emily Brontë, *Wuthering Heights*)

'Pathetic fallacy' means describing natural phenomena as if they have feelings in the same way that humans do. Children can use this device in their narrative descriptions to help depict a mood.

In 'I Wandered Lonely as a Cloud', Wordsworth saw 'a crowd, a host, of golden daffodils', and they were 'tossing their heads in sprightly dance'. This makes them sound as if they are celebratory. Daffodils could perhaps be trumpeting with joy or bowing their trembling heads in sympathy depending on the mood that the writer is trying to convey.

To create this effect, first ask children to describe the actions of humans when they're feeling a particular way. For example, the actions for 'sadness' could include crying, looking down, slumping, weeping and trembling.

Then choose a setting and make a list of items that can be found in that setting. For example, a forest might contain trees, clouds, branches, leaves, a moon, a river, plants and creatures.

Finally, ask the children to describe someone walking through that setting. For example, if the character walking through the forest is sad, then the trees may slump and lower their branches to the ground. The clouds above may weep and the moon may hide its face. These descriptive phrases would help to create a melancholy mood because not only is the protagonist sad, but the whole world around them is also feeling the same way.

Teaching tip

Showing children an image of a setting may be a useful scaffold for this activity.

Bonus idea ★

Read *Wild* by Emily Hughes and discuss with the children the use of pathetic fallacy throughout the book.

IDEA 87

Adding sensory detail

'Nothing revives the past so completely as a smell that was once associated with it.' (Vladimir Nabokov)

When teaching descriptive writing, teachers will often tell their pupils to write so that the reader can create an image in their mind. This image, rather than just being a visual representation of the scene, object or character, becomes more vivid if the reader can place themselves in the moment by imagining not only the sights but the smells, sounds, taste and feel of it too.

Teaching tip

Develop the descriptions by using figurative language to enhance them.

The first step towards developing these rich descriptions is to 'brainstorm' each of the senses around a specific object, setting or character. Even an everyday object such as a pizza can give some interesting results, for example, by asking, 'What does a pizza sound like?' Descriptive phrases that children might come up with here are 'the base cracking as you slice it' or 'the sauce popping as it comes out of the oven'.

Then ask the children to write a paragraph that describes their chosen object, setting or character by referring to the different senses. You could specify that they can't name the object, setting or character – the reader has to guess what it is from the description. For example:

> *The yellow cheese oozed across the base; golden bubbles popped gently as the chef pulled it from the oven. A blast of hot steam escaped and filled the air with the aroma of garlic, herbs and rich tomato sauce. The base cracked as the shiny metal blade cut it into hand-sized slices.*

What would your chocolate factory look like?

'The room was filled from floor to ceiling with jars of peanut butter. On a giant stove, pans were filled with melted chocolate waiting to be poured into the huge copper moulds shaped like squirrels.' (James, Year 4)

In this activity children learn how to write effective descriptions of settings by studying well-known stories. They describe a new setting that would fit well into an established world.

Start by choosing a text that has a number of different settings in it, such as the different rooms in Willy Wonka's chocolate factory, the different rooms in Hogwarts or the magnificent rooms that can be found in *The Nowhere Emporium*, a novel by Ross MacKenzie.

Once children are familiar with the story, choose a number of extracts to compare which describe the different settings. For example, Wonka's factory has a number of different rooms that could be used for comparison, such as the chocolate room, inventing room and testing room. Each room has a different setting with unique and original features and functions.

Whilst studying the range of extracts, teachers may want to point out the key language features – for example, word play or use of similes or lists of items present. Once the children have looked at the descriptions of the rooms, ask them to make notes about the key features. How does each feature make an effective description of a setting? Then ask the children to invent a new, undiscovered room in the chocolate factory such as the Lollypop Room or Fizz Pop Whizz Room. Can they use the same descriptive techniques to describe this new room?

Teaching tip

Some children may be able to create their new setting using Minecraft before describing it.

IDEA 89

Describing a setting, brick by brick

'All my children talk about is Minecraft! How can I incorporate it into my teaching?'

Some children are both reluctant writers *and* reluctant readers – a double whammy when we ask children to read text in order to hook them into writing. It's important that we consider these doubly reluctant children when thinking about writing hooks. In this activity, the hooks are LEGO® and Minecraft.

Teaching tip

In Minecraft, you could restrict the children to a theme, such as challenging them to build a 'Viking' town or a 'futuristic' town. Watching videos of what these towns might look like would then be helpful, such as this video that gives you a 'tour' of a Viking village: www.literacyshed.com/vikingvillage.html.

LEGO has had something of a revival, with many children collecting themed kits. With some investment in kits, you could ask children to create their own landscapes in which their mini figures can have adventures. Children can then write descriptions of the settings, perhaps from the point of view of a LEGO figure.

In 2011, the digital-brick phenomenon that is 'Minecraft' was launched. This brick-based computer game has over 91 million users, with around 50 per cent of all eight- to 13-year olds in the UK playing the game. 'Minecraft: Education Edition' is a version of the game designed for the classroom, providing a 'safe space' for children to build their own worlds which can then be described afterwards.

One idea is to set the children the task of building a house that can then be explored by their classmates. If every child builds a house, this becomes a small town that can be explored by the children. They can then add anything they want to, from town halls to castles, pyramids to graveyards and so much more.

As children explore the class creation, they can make notes and describe the places they see. This can be turned into a piece of descriptive writing.

Description stations

'When I can use other people's words it just makes my writing better!' (Emma, Year 4)

Encourage children to describe settings such as forests, beaches or castles with more detailed description.

In this short extract from *Harry Potter and the Philosopher's Stone* by J. K. Rowling, she doesn't just say 'the castle was x, the castle was y'; she describes various details in the setting:

> *The narrow path had opened suddenly onto the edge of a great black lake. Perched atop a high mountain on the other side, its windows sparkling in the starry sky, was a vast castle with many turrets and towers.*

You can get children to start thinking more about the detail of settings by sharing an image of a setting. Together, collect the key features of the setting. For example, the features of a beach scene might be 'sand', 'sky', 'cliffs', 'rocks' and 'people'.

Write each of these features on large sheets of paper (A2 or A1) and stick them around the room as 'description stations'. Ask the children to use sticky notes to add their own description under each heading. You can add some guidelines to this if necessary, such as asking the children to use expanded noun phrases or similes for some descriptions.

When children have added their ideas to each of the stations, you may want to spend some time allowing the children to read everyone else's ideas and discuss which they find most effective and why. Allow children to choose examples from the stations to use in their own writing.

Teaching tip

Using a collaboration program such as Padlet (www.padlet.com) will allow you to collect these ideas digitally and display them in the classroom when the writing process takes place.

Taking it further

This activity can be used when describing characters too, focusing on physical features and clothing.

Explanation

IDEA 91

Hooks into explanation writing

'I told the class that we would be looking at explanation texts and I got a sea of blank faces, so the next day I told them that we were going to go to Dragon School to become dragon experts and write booklets to explain how a dragon flies.'

Hooking the children into a topic encourages them to want to learn more: to ask questions, spark their creativity and let them lead as learners.

There are many ways to hook the children into the learning. Here are some ideas to explore:

Props: A box with something in it left in the middle of the classroom, a bag with a large sign stating 'do not touch', or a strange item of clothing like a cloak might spark children's interest.

Character: Have an adult dress up and sit in the classroom at the beginning of the lesson. Perhaps leave some clues as to who this person might be. Provide them with a sign which says 'You may ask one question each.'

Question: Provide the children with a question for them to discuss. This could be directly linked to the subject you'd like the children to write about or it could be a completely abstract idea which simply gets the children to begin thinking about giving a series of steps. For example, 'How does a Minion jelly gun work?'

Film: Show the children a film clip, such as 'The Alchemist's Letter' from the Literacy Shed website.

Still image: Distribute an image to the class, such as a hot-air balloon or a volcanic eruption. Ask the children to explain what they think is going on.

Bonus idea ★

Providing the children with an immersive learning experience can really help to hook them into the topic. Ideas such as a staged spaceship crash in the yard or a pop-up planetarium (these can be hired) are amazing ways to enthuse the children about their learning.

IDEA 92

Researching explanation texts

'I realised they had simply regurgitated Wikipedia.'

How do we avoid the situation where the children copy down swathes of research with the addition of a few synonyms and a different title?

To begin, consider exactly what it is that you want the children to research. This may take time to clarify.

Can the children use search engines? Do they understand what happens when different key words are used or if words are used in a different order? Have they been taught about how a search engine orders its results?

Look at skimming and scanning skills. As a class, use texts together to locate vocabulary, identify the gist and assess whether a text will be helpful.

Teach the children about sources and bias. Can the children tell whether the website they're using is a reliable source? Talk to the children about what reasons there might be for a website to be an unreliable source.

Explain the importance of double-checking results. Once the children find the information they need, can they use a second website to verify the results?

Look at note-taking skills. Notes might come in many different forms, such as grids, bullet points and graphic organisers. Ideally, ask children to select the method which suits them best.

Teaching tip

You may need to identify key words to use in searches, or words and sites to avoid. Look at giving the children a question or questions to research as this refines the children's thinking.

Bonus idea ★

Show the children how to 'change and exchange' vocabulary and phrases from their notes so they are considering a different retelling of the information. Talk about which words (usually technical vocabulary) might need to stay the same, but also which phrases might be reordered or use different synonyms.

IDEA 93

Language of explanation

'A three-tiered system of vocabulary can be applied to language and thus enable us to better consider the learning, teaching and application of the vocabulary.' (Isabel Beck and Margaret McKeown)

This activity gives suggestions for helping children learn tier 3 vocabulary.

Teaching tip

Pre-teaching new vocabulary before introducing a text also allows the teacher to gain insight into the level of the children's understanding.

You may have come across the concept of 'tiers' of vocabulary.

- **Tier 1** words are high-frequency words which are used in most children's speech. These are everyday words and require little to no explanation. (For example: 'cold', 'bed', 'sad'.)
- **Tier 2** words are high-frequency words used by mature language users. These words have a direct effect on the comprehension of a text and often involve some explanation when seen for the first time. (For example: 'emerge', 'connect', 'unnerving'.)
- **Tier 3** words are academic words specific to subjects and are used with low frequency. These words should be learned within the context of the subject. (For example: 'cocoon', 'epicentre', 'convection'.)

The subject-specific language found in tier 3 needs to be taught directly so that children can understand the vocabulary they're using and how and why it fits into each context. To do this, teachers need to look at a variety of different methods.

Pre-teach: By introducing and explaining vocabulary in advance, you can make children more aware of the meanings of words before they encounter them in texts.

Vocabulary display: Make and share vocabulary displays, with associated images for words, so that children have a visual reminder to refer to.

Commonality: Look for commonality between words. For example, if writing about how earthquakes occur, investigate the prefix 'epi-' from the word 'epicentre'. Look at other words which begin with 'epi-', such as 'epigraph', 'episode', 'epilogue', 'epidemic' and 'epidermis'.

Repeated use: Can you encourage the children to try using the word in different sentences while keeping the same meaning? Can the word be used in a fiction context?

Glossaries: When studying a topic with children, create a glossary of key terminology with definitions for each word. Encourage children to look at a range of dictionaries to help them decide on the most suitable definitions. Arrange the words on cards on a wall display and keep them in alphabetical order as more are added. This not only supports children's understanding of key vocabulary, but also provides a useful reference point for spelling and discussion.

Bonus idea ★

Play vocabulary bingo with a list of key words during a topic lesson.

IDEA 94

Why aren't doughnuts square?

'Due to the sugary messiness of a doughnut's exterior, the doughnut makers decided that flat sides were too difficult to eat, and, as a result, there'd be too many sticky faces.' (Riaz, Year 6)

It's important that the children understand what a good example of an explanation text should contain. One key feature is the use of conjunctions. A simple way to remind the children to vary their causal conjunctions is to play games with them.

Ask the children to sit facing an interactive board or similar. Show them a grid of eight causal conjunctions, such as: 'as a result', 'consequently', 'because', 'due to', 'since', 'therefore', 'resulting in' and 'for this reason'. Some of this language might need explanation and contextual examples. Look at the fact that these words join clauses or sentences and show that there is a cause-and-effect relationship.

Next, give the class a funny explanation title, such as 'Why aren't doughnuts square?', 'Why doesn't glue stick to the inside of the bottle?' or 'Why do round pizzas come in square boxes?'

Challenge the class to come up with an answer which uses four of the causal conjunctions. Give them a few minutes to jot down their notes and then ask one of the children to come out to the front to give their speech. As they speak, ask the children to note down the causal conjunctions they used. If the children have selected the same four words for their own speech, they can shout 'bingo' (or similar).

Play again but explain that they can only use two of the conjunctions from the first round (so they must use at least two new conjunctions).

Bonus idea ★

Use the conjunction game to also look at conjunctions of time. Swap the 'Why' questions for silly 'How' questions, such as 'How does spaghetti grow?' or 'How do you wash a T-Rex?'

Using fiction for explanations

'We wrote all about how to fly broomsticks because we were reading *Harry Potter* in class. I loved it!' (Alisha, Year 5)

Using fiction texts as a stimulus for non-fiction writing is an excellent way to hook children into writing.

Using a fiction text as a springboard can be an incredibly useful tool when it comes to producing non-fiction pieces of writing. The children needn't learn facts and processes as, often, they are able to create the process themselves. For example, describing the series of steps involved in a volcanic eruption involves learning the science behind the process; describing the series of steps involved in how the BFG's dream blower works can be entirely made up by the children.

To begin, select elements of the fiction text which give the children the most scope to create the content themselves. It can be helpful to provide the children with examples of non-fiction texts which include some of the language they may want to incorporate into their piece. For example, if creating a text about how to fly a broomstick, it may be prudent to look at texts about flight so the children can 'magpie' language and see it in context.

The original fiction text can also be very useful when looking for details which may be essential to the explanation. For example, in *Harry Potter and the Philosopher's Stone*, Chapter 9 gives details about how to fly a broomstick. The book explains how the school's broomsticks vibrate if they're taken too high, it explains how Harry leans forward and points his broom handle down and it explains how to perfect the correct grip – these pieces of information could be added into the explanation.

Teaching tip

Websites such as https://en.wikibooks.org can be extremely useful when gathering extra material for the text.

IDEA 96

Explain the mundane

'We had been reading *Until I Met Dudley* and the children thought the explanation of the dishwasher being full of cats licking the plates was hilarious. From that we began to design household items and explain how they worked.'

The idea of explaining how a mundane, everyday household item works can seem boring and limiting for some children. However, proposing interesting explanations as to how a toilet flushes, how a hairdryer works and what's inside a vacuum cleaner can be incredibly funny and creative.

Teaching tip

Use online printable instruction manuals to find images of items and remove the text so that the children can make notes on how they might work.

Hook the children into the task by watching Wallace and Gromit's short 'Cracking Contraptions' films. Then ask the children to create their own silly explanations for how a household item works. You could start by doing this orally, making recordings of the children's explanations.

Spend some time as a class considering how to write, structure and present an explanation text. Return to the recordings and consider how the children might improve their language choice or structure their sentences differently. Also take some time to consider how they might present their explanation in writing (do they want to include features such as diagrams, text boxes, charts or a glossary?) and how formal they want their writing to be.

The children might benefit from looking at the language associated with the household item, for example, by looking at household catalogues and websites. For instance, take a vacuum cleaner. With a cursory internet search, it's easy to find words like 'debris', 'powerful', 'enhanced', 'upholstery', 'capacity', 'versatile', 'lightweight', 'suction' and 'cylinder'. Children could use some of these in their explanation texts.

Looking at features of explanation texts

'When it came to analysing the text, I found that I was simply doing the same thing over and over again. The kids were bored, I was bored, so we started to come up with new ways to engage them at this point in the writing cycle.'

Coming up with different ways to pull apart a text and study the features of a particular genre is essential in maintaining classroom engagement. Below we have listed different approaches that might work in your classroom.

Three-text comparison: By giving the children three similar texts on the same theme, they can begin to cross-examine which features all three have in common.

Tracing paper: Children love using tracing paper over the top of a piece of text. Use this approach to allow them to make notes onto a book. They can draw arrows, highlight and make side notes.

Cut and jumble: Give out a version of an explanation text which has been cut into several sections. There needs to be an obvious link between paragraphs and sentences. Ask the children to reassemble the text.

Sticker analysis: Provide the children with stickers for some of the features they need to find. Use these on enlarged A3 versions of explanations.

Using annotation software on a tablet: By using annotation software, such as Skitch or Explain Everything, the children can upload or access texts and create annotations about the features of the text.

Teaching tip

'Cut and jumble' works well when looking at causal conjunctions and how they link ideas. How did they know the order of the paragraphs?

Taking it further

Using a points system correlating to a certain number of features can add an element of fun to the lesson.

IDEA 98

Glossaries

'Writing the glossary for the explanation text really helped the children to consider the language they were using. However, I wrongly presumed that they would just understand how to do it.'

Glossaries are a key part of some explanation texts and how to write them is a skill that needs to be taught explicitly.

Begin by exposing the children to texts which feature glossaries. At Key Stage 2, this should not be new learning. Ensure that the children refer to the glossary as they read.

Next, ask the children to consider the language that would need to be explained in a glossary. Give out texts featuring subject-specific, technical language. Ask the children to work systematically through the text to highlight the language they think would need explanation. Clarify with the children why they've selected these words. Then ask the children to put the words that need explaining into alphabetical order.

After this, look at how to develop the definition that goes with each word. A simple yet effective game is to offer three different, but accurate, meanings for the same word. For example, in a text about volcanoes, which would be the most suitable definition of the word 'eruption'?

- The act of starting violently.
- When hot materials from the Earth's interior are thrown out of the volcano. This includes lava, rocks, gas and dust.
- An instance of erupting or ejecting.

The children should be able to see here that the most appropriate would be the middle definition as it gives information which is vital to understanding the text.

Bonus idea ★

Give out glossaries and ask children to try to ascertain from them what the original text could be about. Then ask children to write their own text to accompany the glossary.

A very Christmassy explanation

'During our non-fiction writing topic in December, I wanted to make sure the children were engaged and motivated.'

As mentioned in Idea 95, creating an explanation text about a subject that the children can entirely fabricate themselves can help to maintain their interest and cut out the research stage of some more traditional explanations.

December provides a wealth of opportunities to harness some of the excitement of Christmas: writing explanations about how reindeer fly, how presents are delivered and how to prepare the sleigh for 24 December to name but a few. Hybrid texts – where elements of narrative writing and explanation feature in the piece – could also be used. For example, children might create narrative content about a disaster which nearly befalls Father Christmas when employing new elves.

Here are some ideas for hooks into Christmas-themed writing:

- Use www.noradsanta.org to track Father Christmas from 1 December.
- Use https://santatracker.google.com/village.html for games and activities linked to Christmas and the opportunity to track Father Christmas.
- Use www.literacyshed.com/the-christmas-shed.html for a wealth of film clips and Christmas adverts.
- Use extracts from a Christmas-themed text, such as *A Boy Called Christmas* or *The Girl Who Saved Christmas* by Matt Haig.
- Use https://ifaketextmessage.com to create a series of fake texts between Father Christmas and his elves.

Teaching tip

When considering using Christmas as a subject for explanation texts, children who don't celebrate Christmas need to be considered and planned for. Their explanation texts might be about an element of their own traditions and beliefs or how Christmas is celebrated in their country of birth (if it is).

Bonus idea 

Children might want to produce their explanations in the form of a documentary-style presentation which could be filmed, create explanation articles for a class newspaper about Christmas, or produce a page for a 'Guide to Preparing for Christmas by Father Christmas'.

IDEA 100

Explanation... but not as we know it

'We created mini-documentaries, filmed them and asked parents to come into school for a "screening" with popcorn.'

Oral presentation is often overlooked in favour of a more traditional write-up, yet presenting work orally can be incredibly effective in teaching the use of sentence structures, causal language, tenses, levels of formality, active and passive voice and vocabulary choices.

Teaching tip

Allow the children to film themselves and critically evaluate their presentations before asking them to present their final piece.

Taking it further

Look at how the children need to explain any technical vocabulary used: could their presentation be accompanied by a handout?

Oral presentations could come in the form of a science-fair demonstration or an explanation of a geographical process for a mini-documentary. The children might create presentations as part of a pretend news report about a historical event, as a way of demonstrating their understanding of a creative process (such as how to do batik, a process of printing fabric), or even as a demonstrative explanation for a physical education activity (such as why we need to warm up and cool down).

When presenting an explanation, it's important that the children's opening piece to camera (or their audience) explains what the rest of their presentation is going to be about and leads the viewer to want to know more. Clever layering of questions, elements of persuasion and an emphasis on intriguing the audience into wanting to know more is key ('Surely you're interested in finding out how Tutankhamun's tomb was discovered by...?').

As the piece builds, the use of causal language needs to be applied to demonstrate the links between the elements of the process that the children are explaining. Formality should be discussed, demonstrated and explored.